Tradition and Revolt

Imperial China

Islands of the Rising Sun

Imperial Visions
The Rise and Fall of Empires

Tradition and Revolt

Imperial China

Islands of the Rising Sun

Joyce Milton
Imperial China

Wendy B. Murphy
Islands of the Rising Sun

Preface by Donald H. Shively
Professor of Japanese History and Literature
Harvard University

HBJ Press
a subsidiary of Harcourt Brace Jovanovich
New York, New York

HBJ Press

Publisher, John R. Whitman
Executive Editor, Marcia Heath
Managing Editor, Janice Lemmo
Series Editors: John Radziewicz, Suzanne Stewart
Editorial Production, Debbie Duke, C. Hope Keller

Marketing Staff: Mark Mayer, Jose J. Elizalde, Laurie Farber

Authors: Joyce Milton, Wendy B. Murphy
Picture Researcher, Janet Adams
Assistant Picture Researcher, Lynn Bowdery

Consultants
    Imperial China: Timothy Bradstock
    Islands of the Rising Sun: Judith Rabinovitch

Design Implementation, Designworks

Rizzoli Editore

Authors of the Italian Edition
    Introduction: Professor Ovidio Dallera
    Imperial China: Dr. Giancarlo Costadona
    Islands of the Rising Sun: Professor Ada Caruso
    Maps: Gian Franco Leonardi and Fernando Russo
Idea and Realization, Harry C. Lindinger
Graphic Design, Gerry Valsecchi
General Editorial Supervisor, Ovidio Dallera

© 1980 by Rizzoli Editore
Printed in Italy.

Library of Congress Cataloging in Publication Data

Milton, Joyce.
    Tradition and revolt.

    (Imperial visions ; v. 5)
    Includes index.
    1. China—History.   2. China—Kings and rulers.
3. Japan—History.   4. Japan—Kings and rulers.
I. Murphy, Wendy, B., joint author.   II. Title.
III. Series.
DS735.M555   951   79-2511
ISBN 0-15-004028-8

Contents

Preface

Western civilization developed with little awareness that a world of comparable complexity and sophistication was flourishing on the opposite end of the Eurasian continent. Throughout the four-thousand-year-period that saw Western culture evolve in the Mediterranean basin, spread across Europe, and reach the New World, the civilization of China was very much alive, its influence reaching beyond the boundaries of the Chinese Empire to Japan, Korea, central Asia, Tibet, and Indochina. In fact, the Chinese came to see themselves as inhabitants of the Middle Kingdom (Chung-kuo)—the center of civilization—distinct from what they considered the "barbarians" of the north, south, east, and west. No other civilization has succeeded in maintaining as high a level of cultural integrity and development as China has, century after century, down to the modern age.

The ritual bronze vessels of the Shang dynasty, dating back over three thousand years, are only the most refined of the artifacts that have come to light from that age; such discoveries provide evidence of a long evolution in the arts, technology, political organization, and religious rites of China that had begun centuries earlier. When in the West the Roman Empire was at its height, the powerful Han dynasty extended China's rule from Korea to beyond the Tarim Basin in central Asia. Tang China (seventh and eighth centuries A.D.) was one of the most brilliant empires in history, both in the realm of the arts and in the sweep of its political influence.

The geographical isolation of China from the centers of Western civilization permitted only irregular, tenuous trade contacts until the expansion of European maritime commerce early in the sixteenth century. Trade subsequently increased, but until the twentieth century the West made slow progress in appreciating the rich philosophical traditions of Confucianism and Taoism, China's Buddhist legacy, and the vast repository of historical records and literary texts. Although Chinese accomplishments in sculpture, painting, ceramics, and bronzes were understood more readily by Westerners, knowledge of these cultural achievements too was less than complete. Archaeological finds of the last twenty years have revealed an even richer and more varied culture from the pre-Han to the Tang dynasties than had been previously imagined.

The power of Chinese culture to transmit its values and observances to another society was well demonstrated in Japan. Beginning with the introduction of Chinese writing and Buddhism in the fifth and sixth centuries, Chinese learning and political institutions transformed Japan from a primitive, tribal society to an ardent follower of the Chinese model. The chief of the ruling clan, who claimed descent from the sun goddess Amaterasu of early Japanese mythology, became an "emperor" in the Chinese style, having all the trappings and ritual of the Chinese court and presiding over an elaborate bureaucracy. The Japanese imperial line has continued until the present day—a unique record of unbroken succession.

By the tenth century, enthusiasm for Chinese culture moderated, and elements deeply rooted in native society and psychology began to reassert themselves in the artistic life of the Heian court. The sensitivity of the Japanese to nature, as well as the subtle code of aesthetic taste and social behavior that developed in court circles, were expressed most movingly in short poems (*waka*), diaries, and novels—such as the *Tale of Genji*—written by women of the imperial palace. The effective political power of the country passed from the emperor and court nobles to the newly emergent samurai elite during the twelfth century, and new artistic forms developed as military lords and Buddhist temples became the dominant patrons. In the seventeenth century the appearance of wealthy merchants in the commercial cities led to the flowering of a more popular genre of arts and crafts, a development that reflected the less refined, more colorful taste of the urban commoner.

The ability of the Japanese to maintain old traditions is reflected not only in the continuity of imperial and religious institutions but also in the arts. Despite Japan's rapid westernization in the areas of education and technology during the last century, the country's cultural heritage has been safeguarded generation after generation. Court music and dances, introduced from the mainland continent in the eighth century, are still presented in the imperial court and in Buddhist temples, the *nō* drama of the fifteenth century is widely studied and performed, and the *kabuki* and puppet plays of the seventeenth century are popular forms of drama even today. Japan's success at preserving its traditions, even as it is advancing its stature as a world power, has made the nation a living museum.

DONALD H. SHIVELY
Professor of Japanese History and Literature
Harvard University

Imperial China

In the twelfth century B.C., China was ruled by a tyrant named Chou Hsin, a man whose intelligence and vigor were exceeded only by his talent for finding new and bizarre ways of doing evil. This corrupt king exploited his subjects, imprisoned his virtuous rival Wen Wang, king of the Chou, and once, to satisfy his curiosity about a tradition which held that all sages have seven openings in their hearts, ordered his own uncle slit open and dissected. Eventually, Chou Hsin's misdeeds caused Heaven to withdraw its blessing from his rule. He and his concubine were immolated in the ruins of their fantastic castle, and Heaven's mandate fell to Wu Wang, Wen Wang's son and heir.

Preceding page, a segment of the Great Wall.

Chinese territory extends from the Fragrant Hills near Peking (above left) to the subtropical rice fields of the south (above). The mountains of the northwest (right) have been deeply scarred by erosion of the loess soil. Sediment from this erosion gives the Huang Ho, or Yellow River, its name.

Left, the wasteland of the Gobi Desert, which lies between the northwestern section of the Great Wall and the Mongolian steppes.

For all anyone knows, the tales of Chou Hsin's wickedness may have been invented by Wu Wang and his successors to justify the transfer of power from the Shang dynasty to the new Chou dynasty. Significantly, the Chou chroniclers thought it necessary to demonstrate that the founders of their dynasty had seized power only after it became clear that Heaven had turned its face from the old king. Even at this early date, the Chinese recognized the king's role as intermediary between heaven and earth. Through his own example and attention to religious ceremony as much as by his participation in the work of government, the king–the Son of Heaven–guaranteed the tranquility of the realm.

The authors of the official chronicles evaluated the worthiness of individual rulers, and indeed whole dynasties, according to the state of the nation during the kings' reigns. If there were defeats and natural disasters, for example, then these tragedies reflected the ruling house's fall from virtue. Little attention was paid to the human characteristics that distinguished one ruler from another. There was even a taboo against the use of the king's personal name, and, consequently, most Chinese rulers are remembered today by honorary titles bestowed upon them after death—"reign titles," which refer not to the king

as an individual but to the period of his rule.

But if intimate glimpses into the characters of China's leaders are relatively rare, the stories about the rise and fall of dynasties do reflect the extraordinary continuity of a moral and cultural ideal. The inhabitants of the Middle Kingdom (as China called itself) thought of themselves as the bearers of the only true civilization and believed that they lived literally at the center of the world. The Middle Kingdom was by no means isolated from contacts with foreign peoples, however, and the "barbarians" of one era were likely to become assimilated as the Chinese of a few generations hence.

The first Chinese dynasty to emerge into the light of history was the Shang, the dynasty that ended with Chou Hsin. Far smaller than present-day China, the Shang kingdom was centered in the territory we now know as the provinces of Hopei, Honan, and Shantung. The vast majority of the Shang people were farmers, but the aristocracy was composed of Bronze Age warriors who fought in wheeled chariots and lived in considerable splendor. The Shang people produced fine large bronzes and possessed a written language, some examples of which have survived on fragments of bone and tortoiseshell used by Shang shamans (priests) in divination. Under the Shang, the

11

Chinese worshiped a number of nature spirits and fertility gods and venerated ancestors. The most important god was T'ien, or Heaven, who at that time was personified as the great and powerful king of the sky.

When the Chou chieftains defeated their former masters, the Shang, they decided to administer their newly acquired territory by giving away large fiefs to collateral branches of the ruling family and to their allies. In the beginning the Chou also had a centralized bureaucracy to help govern the kingdom, but in time the influence of the ruling house declined. In 771 B.C., when the Chou's western capital of Changan was sacked by a coalition of feudal lords, the Chou king survived and managed to re-establish his court in the eastern city of Loyang, but the Son of Heaven was no longer able to exercise any effective control of the lands beyond the vicinity of his capital.

One group that throve despite the disintegration of Chou authority was the scholars. In the family-centered religion of the Chou, scholars assumed the position formerly held by Shang shamans. They advised the aristocracy on the proper observance of religious duties and served as tutors for the children of the feudal lords. In the absence of a strong bureaucracy, the scholars' advice became more valued than ever.

Below, a fisherman at a village on the Shantung Peninsula. Bordered by alluvial plains, the lower Yangtze Valley (right) is a rich agricultural region. Below right, bamboo rafts on a tributary of the Yangtze. Following pages, a junk on Tai Hu, a lake in eastern China.

Era of five mythical emperors 2550–2205 B.C.	During this legendary era, five wise emperors supposedly created the first laws and religious rituals, the tools of agriculture and warfare, and the arts.	**Ch'in dynasty** 221–206 B.C.	Shih Huang Ti established himself as the first true Chinese emperor.
Hsia dynasty 2205–1766 B.C.	The Hsia dynasty marked the beginning of China's hereditary monarchies. The oldest archaeological finds in China date from this period.	**Han dynasty** 汉 202 B.C.–A.D. 220	More than any other dynasty, the Han established the patterns of Chinese culture. To this day, the Chinese call themselves "the people of Han." Confucianism was adopted as the state cult under the Han. Foreign trade along the fabled Silk Route to the West flourished, and Buddhism was introduced from India. Iron and salt mining became state monopolies, and the invention of paper stimulated literary production.
Shang dynasty 商 1766–1122 B.C.	The Shang period was a time of rapid technological progress, notable for the appearance of wheeled war chariots, fine bronze castings, and large-scale irrigation works. Religious life was dominated by priests known as shamans, who invented a form of written language for communication with the spirit world. Excavations at the Shang capital of Anyang have revealed large and impressive palaces where this Bronze Age aristocracy lived in considerable luxury.	**Period of the Three Kingdoms** A.D. 220–280	Peasant rebellions and royal feuds brought the collapse of the Han and led to the emergence of three rival states: Wei in the north, Wu in the south, and Shu Han in the west.
Chou dynasty 周 1122–221 B.C.	The reign of the Chou was marked by violent clashes with the northern barbarians and a struggle to open new lands to cultivation. In 771 B.C. the Chou kings were forced to flee their capital of Changan, and a new era, known as the Eastern Chou, began. Centralized authority disintegrated, giving rise to a feudalistic society plagued by continual warfare. The scholar-philosophers, including Confucius, Lao-tse, and Mo Ti, prospered under the patronage of feudal lords during this period.	**Chin dynasty** A.D. 265–439	Wars between the Three Kingdoms, much celebrated in later literature, eventually gave way to a reunification of China under the Chin. This new dynasty could not withstand the pressure of barbarian invasions, and soon all of northern China was overrun.
		Empires of the north and south A.D. 386–589	In the north, a group of barbarians, the Toba, adopted Chinese culture and established a dynasty based on a military aristocracy. The south was still disunited but by no means debilitated. Nanking emerged as a cultural center, and poetry flowered.

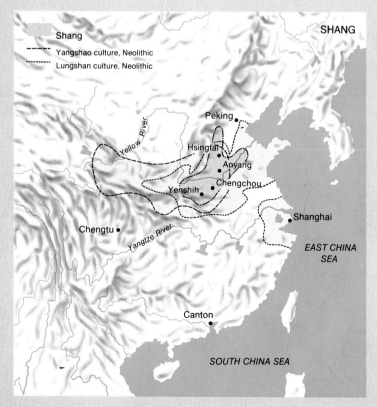

Sui dynasty A.D. 589–618	In 589 a vassal of the Toba revived the imperial power of the Han.	**Yüan dynasty** 元 A.D. 1279–1368	The conquest of China by the Mongols devastated the north and irreparably wounded national pride. During his long reign as emperor, Kublai Khan aspired to win acceptance as a true Son of Heaven and to extend Mongol power by conquering Japan and Indonesia. He succeeded in neither ambition, however.

Sui dynasty

A.D. 589–618

In 589 a vassal of the Toba revived the imperial power of the Han.

Tang dynasty

唐

A.D. 618–907

When the second Sui emperor proved to be extravagant and unstable, his realm fell to the Tang. Their rule brought a golden age of economic and cultural expansion. This was the age in which Li Po and Tu Fu wrote their celebrated poetry, in which printing presses and gunpowder were invented, and in which the first fine porcelain was produced. Changan, the Tang capital, was perhaps the greatest city in the world at this time, with more than one million inhabitants.

The five dynasties and ten kingdoms

A.D. 907–960

The Tang administration eventually overextended itself and collapsed. This led to a power vacuum that was filled in the north by "five dynasties"—actually little more than warlord states. The entire period was characterized by economic disintegration and war.

Sung dynasty

A.D. 960–1279

The founder of the Sung was a Chinese general who accepted the throne reluctantly at the urging of a military cabal. He reunited north and south but was never strong enough to reclaim barbarian-held Peking, and in 1121 the Sung were forced to flee the north and establish a new capital at Hangchow. This was an age of refined artistic tastes and stimulating philosophical debate.

Yüan dynasty

元

A.D. 1279–1368

The conquest of China by the Mongols devastated the north and irreparably wounded national pride. During his long reign as emperor, Kublai Khan aspired to win acceptance as a true Son of Heaven and to extend Mongol power by conquering Japan and Indonesia. He succeeded in neither ambition, however.

Ming dynasty

明

A.D. 1368–1644

Restoration of traditional values was the chief goal of the Ming dynasty. Freed from the Mongols, Peking was rebuilt on a plan reminiscent of the ancient Han and Tang capitals. The scholar bureaucracy gained firm control of the administration and the intellectual life of the empire. Manufacturing industries were developed in the cities, and noteworthy technological progress was made. Naval power reached its height under the Ming.

Ch'ing dynasty

清

A.D. 1644–1912

The Ch'ing, or Manchu, rulers were northern barbarians who had long been exposed to Chinese culture. They met with hostility, especially in the south, but won support among Confucian intellectuals, partly because they were even less disposed to new ideas than the Ming had been. Popular unrest over Chinese capitulations to the Western powers and a desire for increased internal democratization contributed to the dynasty's fall.

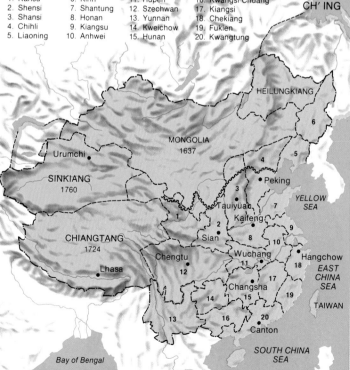

This face of a shaman (left) is among the oldest known representations of the human form. The wide collar suggests that the head may have served as the lid of a mortuary urn. Meats, grains, and sometimes even the bodies of infants were buried in such urns.

Right, a relatively naturalistic head from the prehistoric Lungshan culture of northwestern China. Painted lines on the chin represent a beard.

Among the itinerant scholars of this period was K'ung Fu-tse, or Confucius. Born in about 550 B.C., Confucius never achieved any great renown in his own lifetime, but Confucianism was destined ultimately to emerge as the dominant philosophy guiding government for over two thousand years.

A tutor by profession, Confucius placed special emphasis on the value of moral instruction. Virtue, as he saw it, lay in fulfilling one's proper role in the hierarchies of family and society. "If I am not a man among men," Confucius asked, "then what am I?" His outlook left little room for individualism and none for the concept of human equality. It did, though, emphasize the responsibilities of those in authority: Good government depended on the moral character of the officials, and the ruler who resorted to violence to achieve his ends was counted a failure.

Confucius' disciple Mencius, who lived during the troubled fourth century B.C., was a caustic critic of the corrupt and warlike behavior of the feudal nobility. Because he believed that human nature was basically good, Mencius urged rulers to rely on education and exemplary behavior as tools of power. Mencius' doctrines proved difficult to apply, however, since China's rulers lacked the material resources to provide for the people in the way Mencius prescribed.

Other thinkers of the period outlined different paths to the good society. The fifth-century B.C. philosopher Mo Ti proposed a less family-oriented value system. His advocacy of universal love and brotherhood was a popular subject for nineteenth- and twentieth-century Christian missionaries, who stressed the parallels between Moism and Christian ethics. The Moist school, though, never approached Confucianism in its impact on Chinese thought.

Two other schools of philosophy did prove to be durable rivals of Confucianism. Legalism, as its name implies, considered firm and impartial laws to be more effective than moral suasion. Its teachings were especially popular with pragmatic and energetic rulers, who considered the Confucians to be starry-

Above right, a Shang dynasty ritual vessel in the shape of two owls back to back. Near right, a four-legged rectangular bronze vessel used for cooking food offerings. The essence of such sacrifices was consumed by the gods; worshipers ate the rest. This incised jade tablet (far right) was carried by the king as a symbol of his authority. The piece dates from the Chou dynasty, but the poem seen at the bottom was carved by an eighteenth-century emperor.

細起花文若有神撫無留手卻
平勻知其是玉疑非玉謂此非
珍孰是琭琊合古人餘湯穆華
羞時語詡詡千年邈跡一朝
現巢許寧稱善隱淪
乾隆丙午季春御題

eyed utopians. The second philosophical school, Taoism, is somewhat more difficult to describe. In fact, it is by nature indefinable, since the Taoists taught that mystical revelation, and not reason or book learning, serves as the true path to knowledge.

Taoism's founder, Lao-tse, is said to have been an official in the Chou court who grew disenchanted with public life and retired to a life of contemplation. Although the writings ascribed to Lao-tse were almost certainly pieced together by later disciples, the Taoist view of government might well have originated with a man who had seen too much of officialism. "Ruling a kingdom is like frying a small fish," says the Taoist classic known as the *Tao Te Ching*—in other words, the less done with it the better. The Taoist emphasis on following intuition in all activities eventually became confused with popular superstition and magic, but the Taoist principle of inaction—which is better understood as spontaneity rather than absolute inertness—had an impact on art and literature that extended far beyond the devotees of the vulgarized Taoist sects.

The emergence of so many conflicting solutions to the problem of man's relationship to society reflects the breakdown of order during the last centuries of the Chou. When the rulers of the western principality of Ch'in finally managed to unite the warring Chinese states in the mid-third century B.C., they did so by espousing Legalism, the most authoritarian of these doctrines. Ch'in's hegemony was short-lived (221–206 B.C.), but its accomplishments were substantial. The founder of the Ch'in dynasty, known by his posthumous name of Shih Huang Ti (literally "First Emperor"), is remembered as the creator of the first true Chinese empire.

Shih Huang Ti, celebrated as the "Tiger of Ch'in," was more than just an unusually successful warlord. With the help of Li Ssu, his chief official, he divided the territory he conquered into thirty-six administrative districts, authorized the building of roads, promulgated a uniform system of laws, and even oversaw the standardization of the writing system. To protect

Left, a kneeling woman waiting to attend to the needs of a deceased lord. Excavated in Shensi Province, this pottery tomb figure of the Ch'in dynasty wears a simple kimono-style costume. The bronze funerary figures from the Chou dynasty shown on this page include a pair of wrestlers (below), a panther (below right), and a kneeling servant designed to hold a lamp or censer (right).

the northern frontier against barbarian incursions he ordered the construction of an unbroken wall extending thousands of miles over rugged mountains and through uninhabitable desert—the Great Wall. At home, he is said to have built no fewer than 270 royal palaces. An inscription carved during his reign boasted that "for the first time, he has united the whole world."

Ch'in rule was effective but harsh. Thousands of conscripted laborers must have died while toiling on the Great Wall. Prisoners of war and those who had rebelled against Ch'in supremacy worked in chains, and ordinary peasants were forced to labor under conditions far worse than those they had known at home. Anti-intellectual campaigns were also undertaken during this period. A decree issued by Shih Huang Ti in 213 B.C. ordered scholars to destroy all manuscripts that might be interpreted as challenging Legalism and the supreme authority of the Ch'in. Hundreds of scholars were executed for refusing to give up their beloved books, and hundreds more were

killed simply for being scholars. Yet the decree did not succeed in stamping out Confucianism, despite the fact that it was ruthlessly enforced. Some Confucian manuscripts were buried for safekeeping, and others were later reconstructed, more or less accurately, from memory.

It is difficult to arrive at a balanced assessment of Shih Huang Ti's career. Although in recent times the Chinese Communists have hailed the Tiger of Ch'in as a progressive figure, earlier historians were less complimentary. Shih Huang Ti was often described as a madman whose life was governed by irrational fears and superstitions. A typical story has it that the emperor once attempted to climb a sacred mountain but was deterred by a rainstorm; the outraged ruler ordered the mountain deforested and painted red— the color associated with convicts. Whether Shih Huang Ti was really any more superstitious than other men of his time is hard to assess, but he does appear to have been haunted by a fear of dying. Believing the tales of a magician who claimed to have

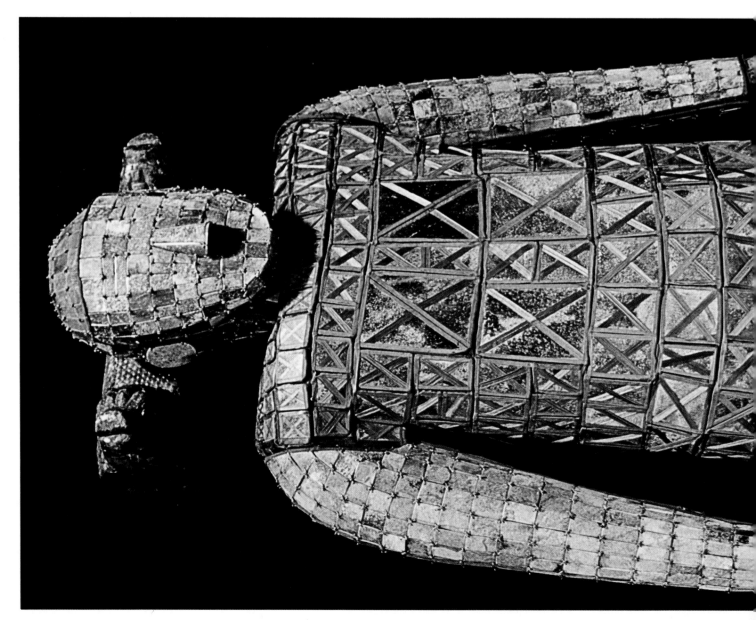

discovered a mushroom that would bring eternal life to anyone who ate it, he equipped two expeditions to search for the elusive fungus. In the later years of his reign, he traveled unceasingly through his domains, sacrificing to local divinities, consulting sorcerers, and avoiding direct contact with potentially discontented subjects.

When death finally caught up with the Tiger of Ch'in in 210 B.C. there was no strong successor to take his place. This unstable situation was successfully exploited by Liu Pang, a peasant's son who began his career as a provincial police official. Sharp witted, favored with excellent advisers and generals, and im-

The Han princess Tou Wan was dressed for eternity in this burial suit (below and detail at left) made of more than two thousand jade pieces sewn together with gold thread. The tomb of Tou Wan and her husband, Prince Liu Sheng, was discovered in 1968. Liu Sheng was devoted to wine, women, and luxury; his more frugal brother became the great emperor Wen Ti.

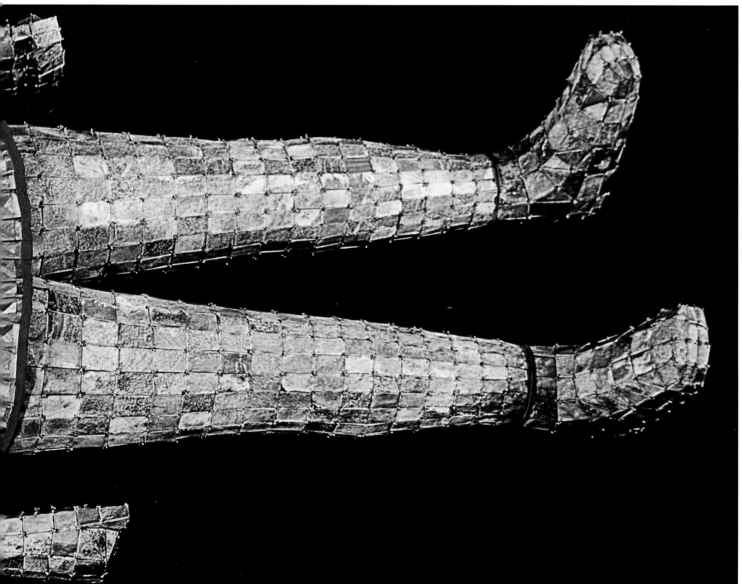

Agriculture

The epic of Chinese civilization has largely been the struggle to bring a vast country under cultivation. This truth was recognized as early as 167 B.C. by the Han emperor Wen Ti: "Agriculture is the foundation of the world. No duty is greater." Peasants ranked above merchants and artisans on the social scale; nevertheless, they led a hard life, battling cold winters and fierce summer droughts.

Land distribution was a continuing problem. Reformers often harked back to the example of the "well-field" system of the early Chou, in which eight families were allotted equal plots of land that were arranged around a ninth plot farmed communally for the benefit of the lord. Scarcity of capital and usurious interest rates led to the formation of some large estates, but the typical farm was kept small. By the twentieth century, holdings of one to three acres were common, and a farm of five acres supported an average of 5.7 persons.

Above, terraced rice fields in eastern Szechwan. Stone terraces prevented soil erosion and increased the cultivable area.

Left, tea processing during the Ming dynasty. Tea leaves were dried in the open air and then roasted in special pans. This primitive well (right) dates from the Ch'ing dynasty.

Right, pressing grapes. The methods of producing wine and distilled spirits have been known since ancient times, and Chinese literature contains many references to the joys of intoxication. Wine was traditionally a drink of the elite classes, and in the modern era the consumption of alcoholic beverages has lagged far behind that of tea.

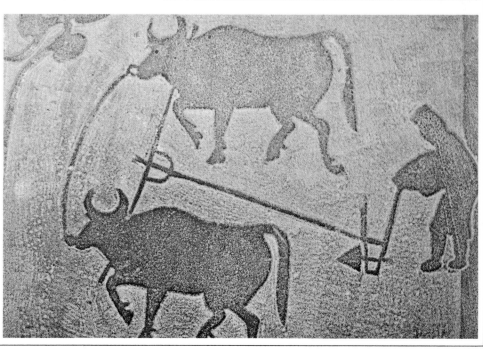

Oxen and water buffaloes have always been the draft animals of China: Their broad hooves make them better suited than horses for plowing muddy fields. Even a passing comparison of this modern photograph (center right) and this Han dynasty stone relief (right) reveals that advances in yoking techniques and plow design have been minimal. Chinese agriculture has remained relatively unmechanized and labor intensive. The widespread use of natural fertilizers has done much to preserve the fertility of the land.

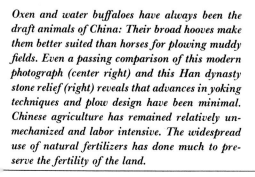

Music

Never merely an entertainment or an art form, Chinese music has always been a reflection of the cosmic order. As one philosopher phrased it: "Music expresses the accord between Heaven and Earth." The origins of musical theory were ascribed to the legendary predynastic period of the "Five Emperors," one of whom is said to have invented the twelve-tone scale by taking six notes from the song of a male phoenix and six from the song of a female phoenix. As this story suggests, the relationship between musical tones was determined by both symbolic and mystical considerations.

The Chou dynasty recognized a further connection between music and government. Confucius, said to be an accomplished performer himself, prescribed music as an integral part of the rituals of the state cult, and when the Ch'in emperor Shih Huang Ti commanded the destruction of Confucian literature, musical instruments were burnt as well. By Tang times, music had again become an important part of court life. Performers were trained at the Imperial Academy of Music, which attracted students from as far away as India and Korea, and noble families typically supported their own troupes of musicians. One imperial Tang court boasted six "standing" and eight "sitting" orchestras.

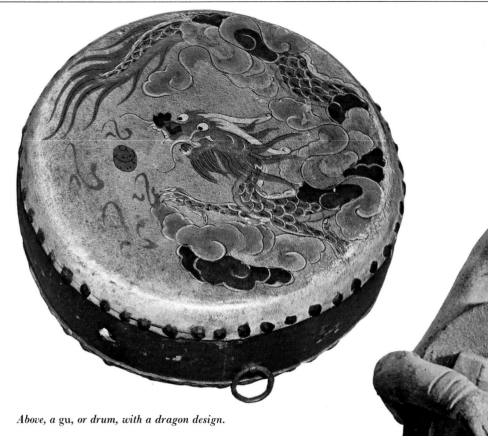

Above, a gu, *or drum, with a dragon design.*

Below, musicians in a Buddhist paradise, depicted in mural decorations from a monastic center founded during the Wei dynasty.

Because of their connection with religious rituals, musical instruments remained relatively unchanged for centuries. Above, a terra-cotta figurine of a Tang dynasty lute player. Right, a mandolinlike instrument used to accompany both classical and country dancing.

Above, a detail of Playing the Lute and Drinking Tea, *a Tang dynasty scroll painted with ink and water colors. Female musicians and entertainers, like this dancing girl (below), were brought from the Chinese provinces, Indochina, Korea, and Turkestan to be trained at the Tang capital of Changan.*

Han tombs

The elaborate tombs of Han nobles, which were constructed of stone or brick with corbeled or barrel vaults, give some idea of the skill of ancient Chinese builders—and an indication of the power of Han rulers to command large-scale forced labor. In addition to pottery models of soldiers, workmen, and servants, Han tombs included rich stores of bronzes, jade and gold objects, lacquered chests, and boxes. Many Han burial vaults, which were typically enclosed in artificial grave mounds, were long ago despoiled, but recent discoveries suggest that there may be more rich finds waiting to be unearthed.

Almost as revealing as Han burial objects are the paintings and relief carvings found on tomb walls. Artists created lively scenes of farm work, salt-mine operations, animal hunting, and the like—all designed to provide comfort and entertainment for the deceased.

mensely popular with the peasants and common soldiers, Liu Pang eventually defeated the other rivals for the Ch'in inheritance and established himself as the founder of the great Han dynasty in 202 B.C. Liu Pang seems to have enjoyed his triumph wholeheartedly. Although he set up his court in the traditional capital of Changan, he feasted with old friends from humbler days at sumptuous banquets during which villagers were encouraged to swap stories about old times with their new emperor. At the height of his power, Liu Pang loved to reminisce about his lowly beginnings, reminding his subjects that "it was while dressed in rough cloth and wielding a three-foot sword that I conquered the empire."

Since Han authority depended on the acquiescence of the landowning class, Liu Pang and his descendants attempted to steer a moderate course between the autocratic policies of the Ch'in and the feudalism of the Chou. The energetic Wu Ti, who became emperor in 157 B.C. and ruled for fifty-seven years, strove to use the scholar class as a bulwark against the ambitions of noble landowners. Somewhat reluctantly, he extended imperial protection to the Confucian philosophers and raised these traditional critics of the throne to positions of power.

Nevertheless, Wu Ti remained a convinced militarist, unimpressed by the pacifist views of the literati. The nomadic Hsiung-nu, or Huns, were still ranged throughout Mongolia, threatening to break through the Great Wall. Rather than content himself with an inconclusive border war, Wu Ti launched an ambitious policy of encirclement. He sent emissaries to the Greco-Indian kingdoms of Sogdiana and Bactria and urged the Scythians to attack the Huns from the west. Wu Ti's armies pushed the Huns back across the Gobi Desert and brought vast territories, including the Tarim Basin of central Asia, under Chinese control. They also completed the subjugation of the province of Canton, which had begun during the reign of the first emperor, Shih Huang Ti.

In this way, the Middle Kingdom gradually expanded beyond its traditional homeland in the plains of the Yellow River Basin and came to embrace

Above left, excavation at a Han tomb. Left, a mythical unicornlike beast carved in wood—evidence of Chinese contacts with non-Chinese peoples of northwestern Asia. Right, a helmeted warrior ready to fling a long-since-vanished spear at the enemy. This terra-cotta figurine from the third century A.D. was found in the tomb of a Han nobleman.

neighboring lands and peoples. Although the Chinese thought of themselves as the only truly civilized people, bringing the gift of culture to the barbarians of the north and west and the aboriginal tribes of the south, there was an inevitable exchange of ideas in both directions. Foreign ways—from the cultivation of rice to the adoption of the naturalistic art styles favored by central Asian and northern peoples—soon became incorporated into the Chinese way of life.

The dynamic policies of Wu Ti made the Han empire rich, but Confucian scholars were strongly critical of the continual foreign wars, condemning them as expensive and useless. The reaction of the Han emperors to the scholars' unsolicited advice is best summarized by a statement attributed to Hsüan Ti, Wu Ti's great grandson. Noting that his dynasty had always lived by a code of conquests, Hsüan Ti complained: "We are no longer living in the times of Chou, the age of government by virtue and education. The literati fail to understand the different needs of different times. They speak always of the virtues of antiquity and the evils of the present age.... How is one to give positions of authority to men living in a utopian world and thus devoid of practical sense?"

Pottery models, intended to make the dead feel at home, provide an invaluable record of everyday life in Han times. Right, a small farmhouse with a baking oven.

Left, a typical peasant's house, with a dog and a keyhole doorway. The unusual shape of the opening was thought to bring good fortune.

In A.D. 9 Confucian ideas had an opportunity to prove their suitability as a basis for government but failed. Taking advantage of the increasingly debauched and corrupt imperial family, the duke Wang Mang, a relative of the empress dowager and an avowed champion of the Confucians, seized the throne and declared himself emperor. Wang Mang ordered the confiscation of large estates and redistributed the land to tax-paying peasants. He sent his officials into the markets to regulate prices and buy up surpluses for use in times of scarcity and also abolished much of the slave traffic. These and other radical reforms led to widespread economic dislocation, which, combined with an extraordinary period of bad weather, caused widespread starvation among the peasantry. Soon an insurgent group, known as the Red Eyebrows because of the way they painted their faces, organized rebellious peasants and began making their way up the Yellow River toward the capital at Changan. By the time the rebels were dispersed, Wang Mang was dead and a Han prince was on the throne once again.

The Confucian-trained bureaucrats who remained after Wang Mang's fall were isolationist, firm in their conviction that China had nothing to gain from foreign possessions and nothing to learn from anyone

Left, a model of a walled tower house showing the overhanging "cloud roofs" and brightly painted façades characteristic of Han architecture. Wealthy residents often retreated to the upper story of such houses in search of solitude. This model, now in the Atkins Museum of Fine Arts in Kansas City, Missouri, is among the finest examples of Han tomb pottery. Above, a country residence with a small tower room.

outside the Middle Kingdom. Nevertheless, foreign trade continued to flourish. Chinese silk reached the Greco-Roman world, and in A.D. 166 an embassy claiming to represent the Roman emperor Marcus Aurelius appeared at Changan. Direct contacts with the West were still the exception, however, and most commerce was conducted through a network of intermediaries.

In the end, the Han dynasty was destroyed from within. A series of weak, short-lived emperors fell under the domination of court eunuchs, who tried to assert their power over the bureaucracy by means of destructive and demoralizing purges. The resulting collapse of civil order led to the rise of the peasant insurgence known as the Yellow Turban rebellion, which was led by a Taoist faith healer. The army stepped in to quell these disorders, and Ts'ao Ts'ao, a particularly powerful and unscrupulous general, took over the reins of government from the last of the Han in A.D. 220.

Ts'ao Ts'ao was unable to control the whole empire, however, and China was divided into three rival kingdoms: Ts'ao Ts'ao's son became the ruler of the Wei Kingdom in the north; a competing military leader formed the Wu Kingdom in the Yangtze Valley and on the southern coast; and the last of the Han princes carved out a third kingdom in Szechwan. The half century of civil strife during this "Three Kingdoms" period has provided the background for innumerable tales and romances.

Below, a Han official in his canopied carriage, preceded by an attendant. Excavated in 1969 from a tomb in Kansu Province, this grouping of bronze figurines is notable for the dramatic posture of the horse and the lightness of the carriage's oversized wheels and umbrella roof.

Above, a bronze statue—probably a bodhisattva—from the Toba-dominated kingdom of the Northern Wei. An astronomical chart (center right) from the same period (A.D. 386–534) shows the sky as it would appear over the Yellow River valley. The chart is bisected by a representation of the Milky Way. Far right, a mounted camel—a frequent subject of works by Northern Wei artists. Near right, a ceramic figure of a Sui dynasty warrior.

This era of romance and adventure—if indeed it was that to those who lived through it—soon gave way to a time of outright turmoil. The Great Wall had long been an effective cultural barrier between, as one Han emperor put it, the "people of the crossbow" to the north and the "wearers of hats and girdles"—the civilized Chinese—to the south. With the collapse of the Han dynasty, however, the Huns began filtering across the frontier once again. In 304 a Hun chieftain who happened to be descended from a Chinese princess declared himself the legitimate heir of the Han. In 311 he marched on the city of Loyang, eliminating the successor to the Wei Kingdom, the Chin dynasty.

The Huns burned cities, drove farmers from their fields, and left behind great areas of depopulated wasteland in what had formerly been a productive agricultural region.

Untold numbers of refugees, especially families of wealth, fled southward into the Yangtze Valley and beyond, where they came into conflict with earlier settlers. Landless, they sought positions in the court of the so-called Eastern Chin Empire, a court formed by members of the Chin dynasty who had escaped the torching of the old northern capitals of Loying and Changan. The north, meanwhile, eventually returned to a semblance of order under the Toba (Northern

Above, a painting from the late fourth century A.D. showing the legendary courage of Lady Feng, who was said to have defended the emperor from an attacking bear. Only two works by the artist, the great Ku K'ai-Chih, are extant.

Wei), a barbarian people of Turkic origins that adopted Chinese ways and defended the country against further waves of nomadic invaders. One of these nomadic tribes, the Avars, eventually reappeared at the gates of Constantinople and continued to threaten European stability until they were decisively defeated by Charlemagne—a ruler whose role in uniting Roman and Frankish cultures has sometimes been compared to that of the Toba emperors in this dark age of Chinese history.

Perhaps the most important development during these four centuries of disunion was the rise of Buddhism. The first Buddhist missionaries had come to China during the late Han dynasty, but it was not until this period of anarchy that the hope of nirvana—an eventual release from the sufferings of this world—came to be a powerful attraction for the Chinese people. In the north, Buddhism was adopted by the Toba, who found the new religion more congenial than Confucianism. In the south, Buddhism made headway because of its superficial resemblance to Taoism—a relationship often vehemently denied by the Taoist.

The Buddhist faith as it came to be practiced in China bore little resemblance to the austere teachings of the Buddha himself. Most Chinese adhered to the

Mahayana, or "Great Vehicle," school of Buddhism, which emphasized universal salvation and compassion for all creatures. For the average Chinese, Buddhism was a religion of temples, holy images, and religious festivals—all of which provided welcome relief from the sober family-centered rituals of Confucianism. A description of a Buddhist procession held in the sixth century in the Toba capital of Loyang dwells happily on the gala atmosphere created by throngs of worshipers carrying colored banners, gilded flowers, and ornamental parasols. "Incense fumes blanketed the street like mist," writes the chronicler, adding that "with troops of monks and elders milling about, and with the ground covered by flowers dropped by the people, a magnificent confusion was the predominant order of the day."

Not everyone was pleased by the wide acceptance of this foreign faith. To the Confucian gentry, the

notion of leaving one's family to seek individual salvation as a celibate monk was profoundly shocking. Hardly less distasteful was the popular devotion shown to Buddhist relics, such as the finger bone of the Buddha, whose display sometimes touched off orgies of self-mutilation and hysterical rounds of competitive alms giving.

The best-known anti-Buddhist tract, written in 819, pointedly denounced the Buddha as a barbarian too uncivilized to recognize the sacred bond between father and son. An edict of 845 states the case even more forthrightly: "The plain fact is that for every man who chooses not to till the soil there are several who will suffer from hunger. For every woman who refuses to make silk there are others who will suffer from cold. Now there is a large number of monks and nuns in this country, all of whom, while not doing any work themselves, have to be clothed and fed." Order-

ing the demolition of temples and the registration of Buddhist monks and nuns as taxpayers, the edict asks indignantly: "How does this small faith from the West dare to challenge our cultural superiority?"

Persecutions of the Buddhists began as early as 574, by which time the Toba Empire had disintegrated, giving rise to two rival states. Among those who sheltered Buddhist monks and nuns in their homes were a high minister of state, Yang Chien, and his devout Buddhist wife. By 580, Yang Chien learned that the emperor, jealous of Yang Chien's great popularity, had threatened to exterminate the minister's whole family. This unpredictable emperor soon died, but Yang Chien seems to have concluded that it was too dangerous to remain a servant of this family. Using his prestigious position as commander of the army, he moved quickly and decisively to eliminate the legitimate ruling house and establish himself as king and

Far left, Emperor Wu Ti, who ruled northern China during the epoch of the Three Kingdoms. Wu Ti was one of thirteen great emperors portrayed on a silk scroll by the seventh-century painter Yen Li-pen. Near left, a porcelain figure of a Tang court dignitary.

Above, a Tang horseman and his groom. This painting, from the Buddhist caves of Tunhwang, is the work of a provincial artist. The emperor T'ai Tsung (right) initiated the expansionist wars that brought China to the peak of its territorial influence.

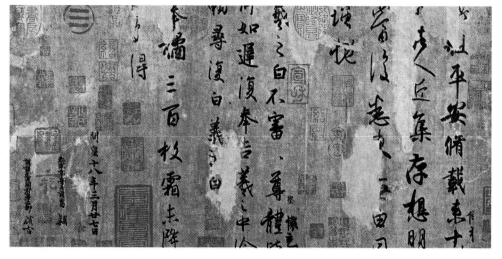

Emperor Hsüan Tsung (left) was driven into exile by the revolt of An Lu-shan. Below, envoys from India, Arabia, and Persia pay tribute to a Tang emperor.

Examples of expert calligraphy (above) were highly valued. This rare fragment by the fourth-century master Wang Hsi-chih bears the red seals of many collectors.

founder of a new dynasty, the Sui.

Yang Chien, later known as Wen Ti, was in some respects comparable to China's first emperor, the redoubtable Tiger of Ch'in. The dynasty he founded lasted only two generations, yet it effected sweeping changes and set the stage for a great era in Chinese history. Yang Chien proved to be an energetic and talented organizer but was plagued by a streak of paranoia. He brooked no opposition from his advisers, and public whippings were common at this court. Not content with reconquering the south, he set out to reorganize the empire along highly centralized lines. He initiated a vigorous foreign policy that spread division and confusion among the newly powerful Turks in Mongolia and built a grand new capital near the site of the devastated Changan.

More Legalist than Confucian in spirit, Yang Chien's administration was harsh, but at least it brought some stability to the countryside. He re-established, for example, the Han system of the "everfull granary"—public storehouses that bought grain in good years and distributed it in times of poor harvests. The inevitable reaction against Sui autocracy did not really gain strength until the accession of the founder's ambitious son Yang Ti. Although he was more sympathetic to the Confucians than his father and sponsored a new edition of the classics, Yang Ti did not fare well at the hands of the historians. The second Sui emperor was said to have had an insatiable appetite for new forms of sexual debauchery and a predeliction for ambitious and expensive projects, including a system of domestic canals and a series of unsuccessful wars in Korea. Like his father, Yang Ti was suspicious by nature. Perhaps, as his enemies claimed, he was also mentally unbalanced, for he is supposed to have become obsessed by the prediction of a fortuneteller that he would be deposed by a man named Li. Rumors spread that the emperor intended to have all officials named Li killed—a serious threat, since Li was (and is) among the most common surnames in China. Li Yüan, a senior general of the Sui army, did not wait to see whether the rumor would prove true. In 617 he moved against the increasingly fragmented Sui regime and a year later was able to declare himself emperor, launching the brilliant Tang dynasty.

Although Li Yüan became the first Tang ruler, it was his talented son Li Shih-min who captured all the glory. A hero in the wars against the Turks and the leader of an expedition to capture the imperial city of Loyang from a rival pretender, Li Shih-min returned home to Changan in triumph. (Even his favorite horse, Autumn Dew, became celebrated in song and legend.) Official histories tell of several attempts by Li Shih-min's two older brothers to eliminate their too-popular sibling. Given poison, Li Shih-min managed to take an antidote and recover; stalked by hired assassins, he learned of the plot through an informer and escaped. When, in the end, the brothers tried to kill him with arrows, they were themselves killed by Li Shih-min and his favorite lieutenant. The emperor, despite his affection for these two eldest sons, forgave Li Shih-min and not long after abdicated in his favor.

The details of this tale may be questionable, but Li Shih-min—known to posterity as T'ai Tsung—did in fact become emperor while his father was still alive. As emperor, he continued to build a reputation as a

Below, maidservants of the Tang imperial court. This pilgrim (below right) is the monk and traveler Hsüan Tsang.

Right, an equestrian tomb figure from the Tang era.

Tunhwang

The belief that the Middle Kingdom had always isolated itself from contacts with foreigners—an idea prevalent among Westerners, who first glimpsed China at the time of the conservative Ming dynasty—was effectively shattered at the turn of this century by the British archaeologist Mark Aurel Stein. Traveling over twenty-five thousand miles on foot through central Asia, Stein reconstructed ancient trading routes that linked the Hellenistic kingdoms, Persia, and the Far East.

Stein's greatest discovery was at Tunhwang, a small frontier oasis that stood at the western end of the Great Wall, where the Silk Road from China proper led into the arid Tarim Basin. Tunhwang was the fabled home of the "Caves of a Thousand Buddhas," artificial rock grottoes dug by Buddhist monks and decorated with religious paintings by provincial artists from the fourth century through the late Tang period. Stein was fortunate enough to win the confidence of a Taoist priest at the grottoes who had been keeping a solitary vigil over an enormous cache of ancient scrolls and painted silk banners. Among the treasures he discovered were Buddhist sutras brought from India by the great Tang pilgrim Hsüan Tsang.

Fortunately, the wall paintings of Tunhwang, filled with mystical visions of Buddhist heavens and valuable information about everyday life, have survived. But many treasures that Stein was unable to purchase were confiscated by Chinese officials, and few have ever been seen again.

military genius, subduing the Turks of Mongolia and Turkestan, reopening trade routes to the West, and bringing the Tarim Basin once again under Chinese control. The Tarim Basin, which has long since been claimed by the encroaching desert, was at the time a thriving cultural crossroads, a stronghold of Buddhism, and the home of flourishing art workshops that brought together Indian, Persian, and post-Hellenistic influences. Thus, T'ai-tsung's conquests both added to the Tang's military security and opened China to new styles and ideas. T'ai Tsung also made the Tibetans Chinese vassals by the end of his reign.

Kao Tsung, the son of T'ai-Tsung, ruled for thirty-three years (650–683) and continued many of his father's policies. Early in his reign, he came under the influence of a beautiful concubine, Wu Tse-t'ien, who had formerly been one of his father's favorites. The scandalous stories told about this woman suggest that her desire for intrigue was unbridled. The best-known tale is that she strangled her own infant daughter so that she could accuse Kao Tsung's empress of the deed. She eventually sidestepped her own son and declared herself emperor and Son of Heaven. Some historians suggest that the empress Wu was actually little more than a figurehead, representing a gentry clique that had grown disenchanted with the Tang practice of allowing Turks and other non-Chinese subjects to gain official positions in government service. In the end, the Turkish leader Bekchor, outraged by the ascendancy of this female usurper, threatened immediate intervention, hastening the empress' demise.

Having lived so long under the domination of his mother, the restored Tang emperor soon became the pawn of his wife, the empress Wei. In 710 the empress poisoned her ineffectual husband to gain sole power, but a palace insurrection foiled her plans. Among the conspirators was a Tang prince who made himself

Above left and left, two details of frescoes in the Buddhist caves at Tunhwang. Above right, Emperor Hsüan Tsung, seen in the lower right-hand corner of this scroll painting, in retreat after the destruction of Changan by rebels. Right, a double row of guardian figures that line the six-hundred-yard-long Spirit Road leading to the tomb of Empress Wu.

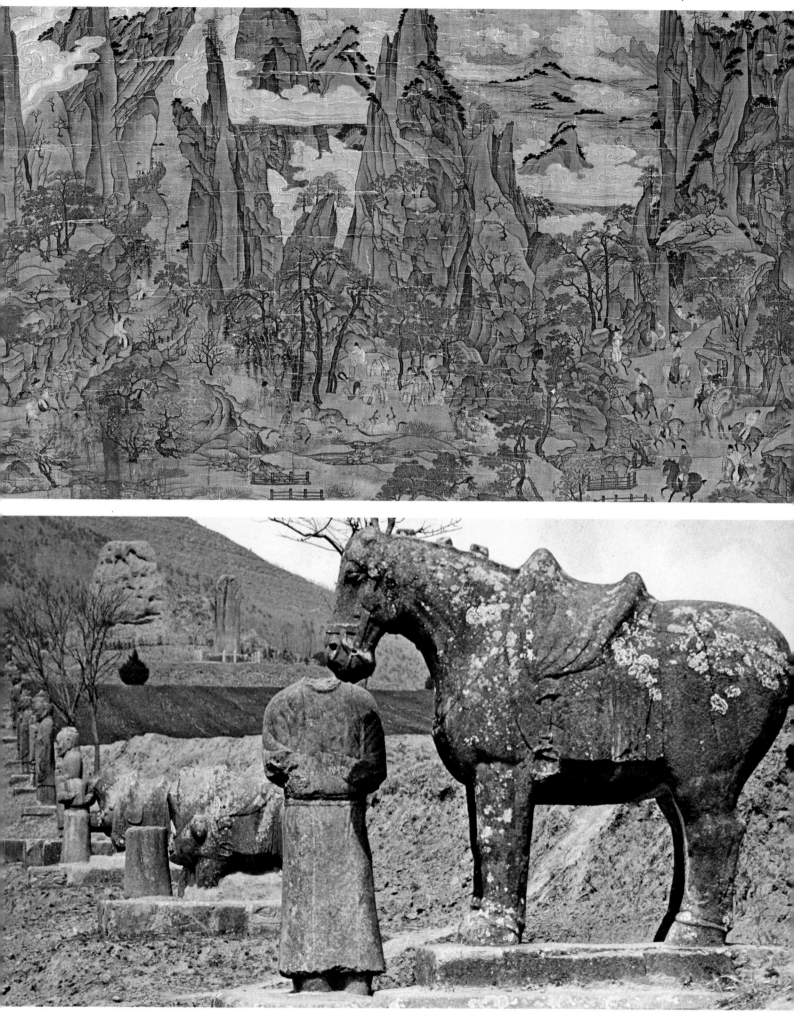

Buddhism

According to legend, Buddhism was introduced into China in the first century A.D. after Emperor Wang Mang saw the Buddha in a dream and sent envoys to India to study the meaning of his vision. Buddhism did not always fare well in China, with some emperors actively supporting the foreign religion and others vigorously persecuting its followers. Nevertheless, Buddhism overcame all obstacles and adapted itself to Chinese culture. Among the typically Chinese varieties of Buddhism is the Ch'an school, better known by its Japanese name, Zen. Far more popular was the Pure Land sect, which promised entrance to paradise to all who had once spoken the sacred name of the Buddha Amitabha.

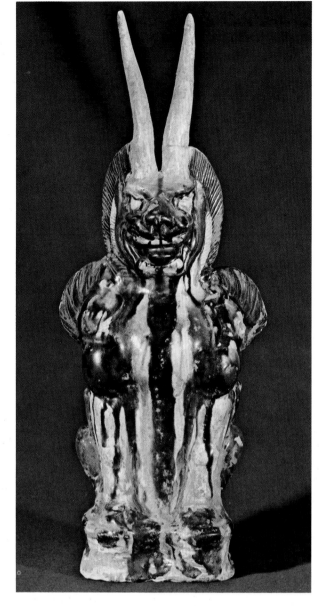

Personifying the spirit of Absolute Nature, the supreme Buddha Vairocana (left) dominates the religious sculptures of the Lungmen caves. The fifty-six-foot figure sits atop a thousand-petaled lotus. Below, a temple guardian frightening away evil spirits.

Above, the god of war—a divinization of Kuan Yü, a celebrated warrior of the Three Kingdoms period. Left, a grotesque monster in polychrome ceramic. The lokapala (below) was a temple guardian assigned to defend the four "Cosmic Directions."

Left, a court entertainment, from a painting on silk now in the Imperial Palace Museum in Peking.

The Tang court

The court of the eighth-century Tang emperor Hsüan Tsung epitomized the cocoon of luxury that effectively insulated emperors—the Sons of Heaven—from the cares of their ordinary subjects. Hsüan Tsung patronized the arts, led royal hunting parties, presided over an endless round of ceremonial pageants—and still had ample time to devote to his favorite concubine, Yang Kuei-fei.

Polo, a sport imported from Persia, was a favorite pastime of the court and was played avidly by women as well as men. In quieter moments, Tang courtiers enjoyed playing cards and board games. Women devoted many hours to cultivating the latest styles in hair and dress. A poem by Tu Fu describes a group of court beauties promenading by the river in "hummingbird headdresses" of iridescent feathers and cloaks studded with seed pearls. "Wrapped in filmy silks bright with peacocks and silver unicorns," wrote Tu Fu, "they illu-mine the spring evening." At home, these noble ladies and their lords lived in villas and palaces with running water and elaborately landscaped gardens.

In 756 the revolt of An Lu-shan brought a sudden end to Hsüan Tsung's idyll. Yang Kuei-fei was strangled in the presence of the distraught emperor, and Hsüan Tsung never fully recovered from the shock of his beloved's death. A romantic song by the poet Po Chü-i celebrates the emperor's love for his murdered favorite: "The span of heaven and the time of earth—they both have their end. But this remorse is everlasting."

Left, the effigy of a faithful servant, waiting to minister to the needs of the deceased. Tang funerary statuettes were cheaply made but nevertheless reflect the vigor and cosmopolitan spirit of the times.

These figurines of stylish Tang ladies (right) were unearthed in a tomb near Loyang in Honan Province.

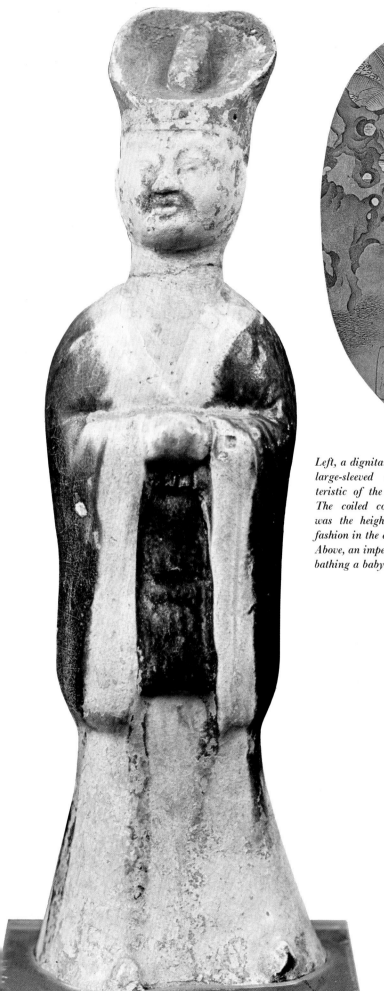

Left, a dignitary wearing the large-sleeved robe characteristic of the Tang period. The coiled coiffure (right) was the height of feminine fashion in the eighth century. Above, an imperial concubine bathing a baby.

In this painting of a lotus flower (above), delicate color and composition take precedence over line. This demanding style found favor with nonacademy painters.

Above, birds and flowers, favorite subjects of the scholar-painters of the Sung dynasty and the specialty of Emperor Hui Tsung. The painters of the imperial academy valued directness and simplicity and regarded elaborate technical effects as suitable only for professional artists.

emperor in 712 and whose reign was to be the apogee of Tang culture.

This prince, known as Hsüan Tsung, was a student of literature, a poet, and a patron of poets, among them the immortal Li Po and Tu Fu. His court was perhaps the most brilliant in all of Chinese history, the product of an era of invigorating cosmopolitanism and stimulating intellectual ferment.

The early Tang emperors exhibited a good deal of religious tolerance. The great T'ai Tsung permitted the practice of Mazdaism, Nestorian Christianity, and other foreign religions, declaring in a famous edict that "the Saints have no fixed abode"—a singular sentiment from the Son of Heaven. Later, the empress Wu, a devout Buddhist, encouraged the growth of monasteries, some of which grew into centers of protocapitalist activity. The freer religious atmosphere helped make Tang culture notably pluralistic. For example, court landscape painters, including the famous Wu Tao-hsüan (who is said to

have passed from this life by disappearing through a door in one of his own paintings) made liberal use of Buddhist and Taoist themes.

Literature too flourished under the Tang. Li Po, whose feckless Bohemian existence makes him a kindred spirit to the romantic poets of nineteenth-century Europe, was the most outstanding poet of the era. He maintained that content and clarity were to be valued above academic perfection of meter and form and is said to have read his works to an old peasant woman, deleting any lines that she did not understand. Although this story is probably apocryphal, it is true that Li Po's works are among the most widely read in all of Chinese literature.

Tang literature reflects a growing popular dissatisfaction with the emperor's expansionist foreign policy. The war poetry of Li Po contains bitter denunciations of Tang conscription. "Three hundred and sixty thousand men, dragged from their homes, weep as they bid their families farewell," he wrote. "Since it is the order of the prince, they must obey. But who is to cultivate the fields?" Tu Fu also protested against the continual warfare, and one of his *Frontier Songs* ends with the lines: "In killing men, also, there are limits, / And each state has its own borders. / So long as invasion can be curbed, / What's the use of much killing?" Nor did the contrast between the luxuries of the court and the miserable lot of the common people escape Tu Fu's notice. One of his poems ends with this stark image: "In crimson gates a stink of meat and wine; on the roadsides lie the bones of frozen men."

Left, Avalokitesvara, the Bodhisattva of the Light, was gradually transformed into the Chinese goddess of mercy, Kuan-yin. By the Sung period, Buddhist art appealed primarily to the lower classes.

Genre scenes depicting schoolboys playing a prank on their sleeping teacher (above) and a puppet theater (below) reveal a livelier side of Sung painting.

Both poets lived to see Hsüan Tsung driven from his capital by the revolt of An Lu-shan, a Tatar general who had once been a confidant of the emperor he deposed. Putting down this revolt, which lasted from 755 to 763, proved even more costly than the Tang's foreign adventures because of the disruption that was caused to the agricultural system. Agriculture under the Tang was based on a system of government allotments to the peasants. Some of the land was granted in perpetuity, but most was held only for the peasant's lifetime. In theory at least, land holdings were distributed more or less equally. This system could be maintained only as long as the bureaucracy was well organized and honest and the burdens of taxation at least kept to bearable levels. Once the Tang set about crushing the civil wars that followed An Lu-shan's uprising, taxes became so heavy that the law against

Left, a detail from the caves of Tunhwang showing an elegant lady making an offering at a Buddhist shrine.

selling land could no longer be enforced. Peasants sold their fields to large landowners and were reduced to tenants.

Significantly, the uprising that finally succeeded in putting an end to the Tang dynasty was organized by a salt trader who had become embittered by the forced loans and humiliating restriction imposed upon merchants. To this extent, at least, the Tang were the victims of their own prosperity, which created expectations that could not be fulfilled under the old Confucian class system. The period between the fall of the last Tang emperor in 907 and the emergence of the Sung dynasty in 960 is known as the age of "Five Dynasties and Ten Kingdoms," the dynasties being in the north and the kingdoms in southern China. But more important than the confused political events of this period were the social changes that caused some old families to become impoverished and allowed new gentry families to rise to prominence. Even though commerce was still considered a nonproductive diversion of energies better used for farming, China now had a money economy, and traders were no longer the itinerant peddlers of olden times. Gentry families speculated in currency or sought out investment opportunities; some even resorted to elaborate tax-evasion schemes. Under the Sung dynasty, some merchants were eventually able to organize regional trade associations, and iron and steel mills, textile factories, and pottery works were established. The prejudice against businessmen remained strong, however, and those in commerce were still denied social respectability.

The founder of the Sung dynasty, T'ai Tsu, was a general in the service of one of the northern dynasties who accepted the imperial throne reluctantly. As emperor, he was conciliatory toward defeated enemies and strove to prevent wars of unification from inflicting suffering on the civilian population. The dynasty T'ai Tsu established may not have been outstanding from a military point of view, but it conformed admirably to the Confucian standard of government and won a lasting place in the hearts of the Chinese people.

Later emperors of the Sung dynasty were patrons of art, literature, and philosophical debate, gentlemen who lacked the autocratic temperament and drive for conquest that characterized their historical predecessors. Under their rule, Chinese thought and society assumed the patterns that were to carry the Middle Kingdom into the modern era.

Sung China paid a price for its military weakness. Its armies were never able to recapture Peking from the Khitan, who had seized the city in 963, and an inept attempt to accomplish the same goal through

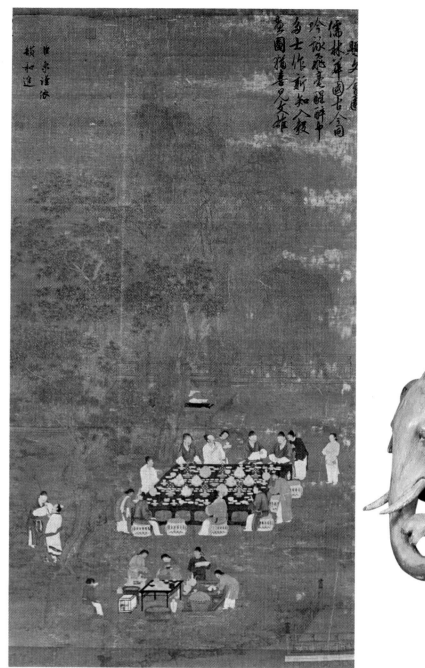

Banquet *(above), a painting on silk, has sometimes been attributed to Emperor Hui Tsung. Right, a detail of a Taoist procession, from a scroll dated 1157. Above right, a gilded wood statuette of a bodhisattva seated on the Sacred Elephant of Good Rule. Following pages, tablets from a twelfth-century book, carved on wood with Buddhist illustrations.*

Horses

Throughout their long history, the Chinese have found little to envy in the possessions of foreign nations. One of the few things foreign that they actually sought out was the Fergana horse, fabled in art and literature as "the horse that sweated blood." The inferiority of China's indigenous horses, typically short legged and heavy bodied, became clear during the course of Han engagements with the cavalry of the Huns. In 102 B.C. a Han commander led sixty thousand men on an audacious march across the Tarim Basin and forced the kingdom of Fergana to agree to an annual tribute of fine horses. These steeds, of Persian origin and known to the Greeks as "Nicaean stallions," were henceforth bred throughout China at thirty-six stud farms established by imperial order.

The "flying horse" (above), discovered in 1969, has become the most celebrated masterpiece of Han art. One hoof rests on the stylized form of a swallow with wings outstretched, reinforcing the impression of the horse's almost magical lightness.

Below, a bronze battle chariot, excavated in Kansu Province.

Horses at Pasture *(right) is the work of Chao Meng-fu, a Chinese artist and calligrapher who served at the court of Kublai Khan. The Mongols were dedicated horse fanciers, and Yüan artists produced many paintings of their heavy-bodied steeds.*

"Dragon steeds" descended from Fergana stock were among the most prized possessions of Tang dynasty noblemen. Equestrian statuettes like this mounted hunter (far left) and this richly caparisoned show horse (left) were produced with exceptional care and attention to detail.

"To live in this world the proper thing to do is to get drunk. To serve as a district magistrate invites only humiliation." So, in part, reads the inscription on this scroll (above), entitled **Home Again.**

diplomacy led to a disastrous alliance with the Ju-chen, who were eventually able to occupy the whole of northern China. The Sung were thus driven from the ancestral home of Middle Kingdom civilization.

Despite these reverses, the Sung period was a time of considerable prosperity and great intellectual accomplishment. The examination system for entrance into the civil service was greatly expanded, bringing new blood into the bureaucracy at the expense of the old gentry class. Confucianism once more became the guiding ideology of the imperial administration, but both the philosophical basis of Confucian ideals and their application to government were energetically debated.

Intense argument was generated by a set of reforms proposed by one Wang An-shih, an eccentric Mandarin who was criticized as much for his sloppy attire and unwashed face as for his unorthodox ideas. In essence, Wang advocated reorganizing the imperial administration along the lines of a welfare state. Some of his proposals, including the elimination of conscripted labor and the establishment of public schools, hospitals, and cemeteries, were motivated by compassion for the common people. But like his Han dynasty predecessor Wang Mang, Wang appears to

have been most eager to promote fiscal stability and to limit the powers of the great landlords. Outright redistribution of land was no longer a feasible goal, but his program advocated tax reform to limit the accumulation of wealth and strict government control of the marketplace.

Wang also suggested changing the content of the state civil-service examinations so that candidates would be judged less on literary style than on their grasp of the duties of officialdom. This proposal revived an old debate over the societal merits of generalists versus specialists. Long before, Confucius had argued for the nonspecialist in public life, declaring

泉明歸去
賦清解字
傲吏謝謝
公知千載
陵名備稱也

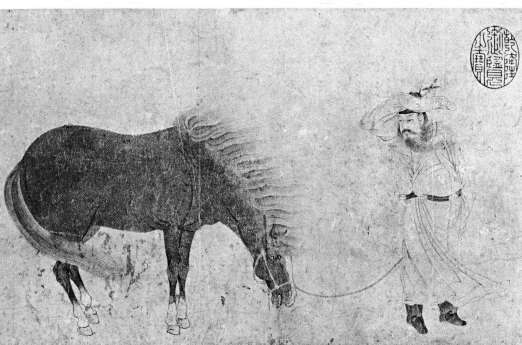

Left, Kublai Khan, the Mongol ruler who aspired to become a true Son of Heaven.

The harshness of the northern Chinese winter is captured in this masterpiece (right) by Chao Meng-fu.

that "the gentleman is not a utensil." But by Sung times, as it became clear that success in the examination had less to do with the intellectual distinction of "gentlemen" than with the mastery of certain academic essay forms, the case for trained specialists became stronger.

Wang's proposals were tried between 1069 and 1085 and during later periods of Sung rule, but the system on the whole never gained the sustained support it needed for a fair trial. Some aspects of the program, including certain public welfare provisions, did become part of imperial policy, but the notion of effecting fundamental changes in the examination system was too much for conservative Confucians to accept.

By the first quarter of the twelfth century, the great debate over social reform was eclipsed by concern over foreign policy. Hui Tsung, emperor since the year 1100, was a highly cultured man whose chief interest in life was judging painting contests. Hui Tsung was himself an accomplished painter, but he had no head for affairs of state. Having encouraged the savage and primitive Juchen to make war on the Khitan, who were by then quite settled in Peking and a threat to no one, the emperor watched helplessly as his new allies made their way southward and set up a blockade around the Sung capital of Kaifeng. This distressing situation led Hui Tsung to the irrelevant conclusion that certain changes made by Wang An-shih in the syllabus for the imperial examinations must have been at fault, and while the Juchen closed around him he spent his time considering a restoration of the old format. When the emperor finally agreed to abdicate in 1125 in favor of his son, it was already too late. Northern China fell to the invaders, and both the former emperor and his son were carried off into the forests of Manchuria, where they died in exile.

In the meantime, one of Hui Tsung's sons, Kao Tsung, escaped the Juchen and re-established the Sung court in the southern city of Hangchow. The new capital soon became even more of an artistic and literary center than Kaifeng had been. Sporadic warfare with the Juchen continued, but Kao Tsung made no concerted attempt to regain the northern territories, preferring to pacify his enemies with tribute offerings.

The once alien south was thus transformed into the center of the Middle Kingdom. But this was only one of the sweeping changes that marked the Sung era. Internal trade increased greatly, enabling various localities to specialize in the buying and selling of ag-

No one, not even the emperor himself, was permitted to travel the Spirit Road leading to the Ming dynasty burial ground except on foot—and then only on the most solemn occasions. The avenue (above) is lined with monumental guardian figures, such as the camel (left), the warrior (near right), the lion (far right), and the court official (above right). The construction of a traditionally designed imperial cemetery only thirty miles from the former seat of Mongol power at Peking was a symbolic victory for the dynasty's goal of national restoration.

ricultural products and handicrafts; in this way, a number of new urban centers emerged. Foreign trade also underwent significant changes. With the severing of caravan routes between China and the West, the Sung were forced to look to the sea. For the first time, China became a seafaring trading power, and the Sung later invited foreign merchants to trade at Chinese ports.

Printing, first developed under the Tang, made books more accessible and stimulated the creation of new literary works. Texts on astronomy, medicine, and botany were produced, but questions about human nature and the proper relationship between man and society still continued to dominate intellectual life. Through the Ch'an (Zen) sect, Buddhism gained influence among the literati, with a number of Neo-Confucian scholars trying to reconcile the Ch'an emphasis on meditation and sudden enlightenment with their own rationalist philosophy.

In general, the Sung dynasty offered more scope for individual freedom and the unfettered exchange of ideas than any dynasty before it. But there were two key groups that did not benefit: peasants and women. The peasants fared no better under the Sung than under the late Tang since they were still subject to the large landowners. The condition of women actually

Porcelain

Porcelain was fired in special kilns (above) capable of reaching temperatures as high as 2,400 degrees Fahrenheit. Hand wheels (below) were used for modeling the kaolin and clay paste. Facing page, below left, finished wares being packed in cylinders made of rush.

In the year 851, an Arabic geographer quoted a report by a Moslem merchant who had visited Canton that the people there owned bowls "as fine as glass drinking cups." The bowls this merchant so admired where made of porcelain, a substance not successfully produced in Europe until 1709.

The development of porcelain was unquestionably the greatest achievement of Chinese ceramicists. Experts disagree on the date of the first true porcelain, but as early as the Tang dynasty connoisseurs recommended that tea be drunk from fine Yüeh-ware bowls, whose translucence was compared to that of jade and ice. A number of refinements were introduced during the Sung and Yüan dynasties, including techniques for applying decorative moldings and beadwork reliefs. By the fifteenth century, fine ceramics were typically produced at large imperial factories. Work at these factories grew increasingly specialized, with one worker, for example, sketching designs, another adding floral motifs, and a third applying color.

The austere and elegant works of the Sung period are considered by many collectors to be the epitome of the ceramicist's art. Delicate figurines of pure white porcelain, as well as stoneware vases with seductively simple shapes and subtle monochrome glazes, were produced during this era to appeal to the educated tastes of the elite. But the less severe and far better known ceramics of the Ming period are by no means inferior. The first pieces of this blue-and-white Ming ware reached Western markets in about 1600. Unfortunately, more and more European buyers requested that their suppliers copy Western designs, and the vogue for "chinoiserie" eventually led to the debasement of the age-old traditions of the Chinese potter.

Right, a Ming vase in the "five-colors" style with a characteristic "cloud neck."

Above, a porcelain vase on a stem from the Ch'eng-hua period, ca. 1465. Below, a ten-sided bowl decorated with floral motifs.

worsened during this era. Concubinage and multiple marriages became more common in the south than they had ever been in the north. There was more prejudice against the remarriage of widows and, with the population swiftly increasing, more pressure for female infanticide. For upper-class women, the most tragic development of the period was the introduction of the practice of foot binding. For the sake of erotic appeal, the feet of young girls were encased in tight, excruciatingly painful bandages. The "lily foot" was a status symbol, since no family that depended on its women for labor of any kind could afford such a crippling practice. By the time they were in their midteens, well-brought-up Chinese women could do no more than waddle along on the supporting arms of their servants: Their feet were hideously deformed, with broken arches, bent toes, and swollen ankles.

Generally speaking, expressions of Sung taste upheld an ideal of refinement and subtlety. In painting and pottery, the Sung avoided bright colors, preferring fine graduations of tints or abandoning color contrasts altogether for monochromes. In intellectual matters, they were less interested in bold new ideas than in the synthesis of the heritage of earlier dynas-

Above left, a view of an ornamental bridge in the garden of the Summer Palace near Peking. Above right, an ivory figure of T'ien Lung, the Lord of Heaven.

The structures in the park of the Temple of Heaven in Peking are Ch'ing restorations of fifteenth-century work. The principal building (right) has an enameled tile ceiling (top left) that rests on columns towering some 125 feet above the heads of worshipers.

ties and movements. Nevertheless, Sung culture was vital and energetic, and there is no telling what might have resulted if China had been blessed with peace. Unfortunately, the Sung flowering ended abruptly with the worst disaster that had yet befallen the Middle Kingdom: conquest by a most formidable "barbarian" people—the Mongols of Genghis Khan.

Although the story of this era, known in Chinese history as the Yüan dynasty, properly belongs to the saga of the Mongol Empire, the future course of the Middle Kingdom cannot be understood without some reference to the impact of the century-long Mongol hegemony. The Mongols were a nomadic people who first became a threat to the Juchen kingdom to the north in about 1210. In the beginning, they wantonly destroyed farmland, turning whole regions back to pasturage. But one northerner, Ye-lü Ch'u-ts'ai, who saw the Mongols as liberators, demonstrated to Genghis Khan that the Mongols could become far richer by establishing a system of taxation than by simply plundering and destroying.

The Mongol khan, who may have been uncivilized by Chinese standards, was nonetheless highly intelligent and adaptable and followed Ye-lü Ch'u-ts'ai's counsel. His grandson Kublai Khan, who ascended the throne in 1260 when he was already in his forties, went much further. Regarding himself as a true Son of Heaven, he resolved to govern in the Chinese manner. In spite of the weakness of the later Sung emperors, however, it was not easy for Kublai Khan to realize his ambition of becoming the sole and universally recognized emperor, the receiver of Heaven's mandate. Loyal Sung officials put up strong resistance over a twenty-year period until they were finally reduced to hiding out in ships off the Chinese coast. In 1279 the flagship of the last Sung emperor, a boy only eight years old, was surrounded by Mongol vessels. A defiant servant clasped the child in his arms and leaped into the sea rather than submit, and thus Kublai Khan became the undisputed ruler of China.

Kublai Khan governed China from Cambaluc, on the site of present-day Peking. He promulgated a law against the destruction of crops by Mongol horsemen, improved the network of imperial roads, and introduced the first kingdomwide system of paper currency. The Mongols' ministers of finance eventually came to issue so much of their mulberry-paper money, however, that the currency became almost worthless.

Although Chinese in form, the imperial government of the Yüan dynasty was staffed mostly by non-Chinese personnel. Some Sung officials had retired from public life rather than serve the new regime, and, in any case, the Mongols preferred ethnic mi-

Left, a nineteenth-century view of Lhasa and the palace monastery of Potala, the residence of the Dalai Lama. Military and cultural contacts between the Chinese and the Tibetans date back to Tang times, when the latter were still a nomadic people. Tibetan Lamaism, a fusion of Buddhism and the native Bon cult, was adopted by many Mongols during the Yüan dynasty. Tibet did not come under Chinese rule until 1720, during the reign of K'ang-hsi.

This Jesuit-made map (above) was only a preliminary to the much more ambitious project that produced the first detailed survey of Chinese territory. Finished in 1717, the Jesuit atlas was 120 pages long and charted a million square miles of land. The Jesuit Matteo Ricci (below), a gifted scholar, compiled the first Mandarin-Portuguese dictionary. Ricci's fluency in Mandarin was widely admired by Chinese scholars.

The Forbidden City

The proper place for a Son of Heaven was at the symbolic center of the world. This conviction was expressed in the Forbidden City, whose design was dictated by astronomical and ceremonial considerations. All who were privileged to enter into the emperor's presence passed through to the walled "city" by means of a series of gates arranged along the north-south meridian. Three throne rooms, each reserved for specific ceremonial functions, stood at the center of the palace complex.

Built between 1409 and 1421 by order of the Ming emperor Yung Lo, the Forbidden City was the centerpiece of a rebuilt Peking—a city not long before liberated from more than four centuries of Juchen and Mongol rule. Yung Lo's dependence on eunuchs, socially despised but a frequent practice in the imperial court, had serious consequences for the future of the Ming dynasty and its new capital. Pampered and overindulged by court life, Ming rulers soon lost touch with their responsibilities. A treacherous eunuch betrayed Peking to the Mongols in 1644, causing the reigning emperor to hang himself from a locust tree on a hill just overlooking the Forbidden City.

The walls and gates of the Purple Forbidden City were painted the reddish-purple hue associated with the North Star. This gate (above) leads to a courtyard containing gardens and a library. Near right, a palace overlooking the Hall of Supreme Harmony, where the emperor's chief throne room was located. The population of the Forbidden City was made up largely of eunuchs and imperial concubines. Many of the latter never served the emperor personally and were celibate.

Above, a detail from the Wall of Nine Dragons. The ceramic tile beasts were believed to protect the imperial sanctuary from evil spirits. Right, the Gate of Great Harmony, as it appeared in the nineteenth century. The gate faced south, the direction in which most of the Chinese Kingdom lay; the emperor thus kept a symbolic eye on his realm.

Clockwise from top right, a sloping ramp, along which the emperor was carried to the throne room; a gilded, fierce-looking bronze lion; the Canal of Golden Waters, crossed by five bridges symbolizing the Taoist virtues; and a bronze censer.

Above, the Hill of Millenary Longevity, which overlooks Lake Kunming, an artificial body of water. At its summit stands the pagoda of the Fragrant Buddha (right), containing statues of the Enlightened One and his disciples.

This page, far right, a covered walkway along the shore of Lake Kunming. The walls were decorated with small frescoes of mythological scenes (below) or with landscapes that recalled the scenery of the old capital of Hangchow.

The Summer Palace

Although their attachment to their northern homeland never diminished, the Manchu emperors were by no means immune to the spell cast by the luxuriant scenery of the old southern capital of Hangchow. Inspired by the gardens and mountains of the Hangchow region and designed with the help of Jesuit missionaries—who added their own Italianate touches—the Summer Palace of the Ch'ing rulers was a unique pleasure garden. Only a few miles from Peking, the Yüan Ming Yüan (Garden of Perfection and Light) contained miles of manmade canals and stone formations, plantings of gardenias, jasmine, and azaleas, and more than two hundred pavilions, halls, and ornamental fountains—all artfully contrived to create an illusion of rusticity.

In 1860 the Yüan Ming Yüan was destroyed by the British in retaliation for a minor truce violation. The dowager empress, Tz'u Hsi, promptly ordered the construction of a new Summer Palace nearby, adding such extravagant touches as a pavilion with a marble boat copied after a Mississippi paddle-wheel steamer. Ironically, the funds for this building project were embezzled from monies intended for the imperial navy.

The gardens of the Summer Palace (above), called by the empress Tz'u Hsi "The Park Where Harmony Is Cultivated," have been open to the public since 1924. Today, the canals are used for rowing in the summer and ice-skating in the winter.

Right, an ornamental wood gate decorated with geometric designs. The figures at the corners of the sloping roofs are monsters designed to ward off malignant spirits.

norities. The ruling elite was, of course, Mongol, but even in lesser offices foreign-born Moslems and descendants of barbarians who had long been in contact with the Chinese tended to predominate. Nationalist sentiment smoldered, but under the wise and generally humane rule of Kublai Khan there was little agitation for large-scale rebellion. But by the fourteenth century matters had changed. Financial disarray and factional quarrels provided the opportunity for revolution—an opportunity that was seized by a certain Chu Yüan-chang, the orphaned son of a poor peasant family. Chu's rebel warriors managed to win the loyalty of the people of the countryside and by 1368 were able to march on Peking, driving the last degenerate descendants of the great Genghis Khan back to their Mongolian homeland.

Chu Yüan-chang, a bandit chieftain, thus became the founder of a new dynasty, the Ming. Having driven out the foreigners, the new Son of Heaven now made it his mission to wipe out all traces of their former presence. He and his son Yung Lo set the tone for a three-hundred-year period of ideological conser-

vatism and political reunification. Although the Confucian literati were now restored to their former positions of influence, both of these early Ming emperors were strong, absolutist rulers. When scholars and officials persisted in the traditional function of criticizing imperial policies, the first Ming emperor abolished the central administrative organ of past dynasties, the Imperial Secretariat, and ordered the execution of recalcitrant bureaucrats and their entire families. In effect, the emperor now ruled almost single-handedly.

Under the conservative Ming, China's scholars and officials became increasingly rigid in outlook. The primary hurdle in the imperial examinations was by this time the notorious "eight-legged essay," a technical form that required years of study. Although there was more social mobility than in previous eras, success in the examinations was in practice limited to those who could afford tutors and the leisure to spend years in study. The pressure on the candidates, who recognized that passing could mean power and liberation from a lifetime of labor, was intense. For the provincial examinations—the second part of a three-part battery of tests—candidates were required to bring bedding and food; after being searched from head to toe for forbidden notes or crib sheets, they were locked up in individual cells for three days and three nights to complete their essays. "Parents, however much they love a child, have not the power to place him among the chosen few," wrote one poet. "Only the examiner can bring the young to notice, / And out of the darkness carry them to Heaven."

Below, an imperial procession to celebrate the sixtieth birthday of the great emperor K'anghsi. The rigid etiquette of the court amazed and perplexed Westerners and sometimes touched off diplomatic crises when European ambassadors refused to perform the kowtow.

Ch'ien Lung (top left), emperor from 1736 to 1796, presided over the Manchu state at the apex of its extent and power. In 1793 the emperor consented to receive an English envoy, Lord Macartney, but only as an "Ambassador bearing tribute from the Country of England." Left, Ch'ien Lung's carved wood throne, now in the Victoria and Albert Museum in London. Top right, Taoist magicians, from a porcelain plate of the K'ang-hsi period. Immediately above, a detail of a painted scroll, Forty-two Poets of the Orchid Pavilion.

69

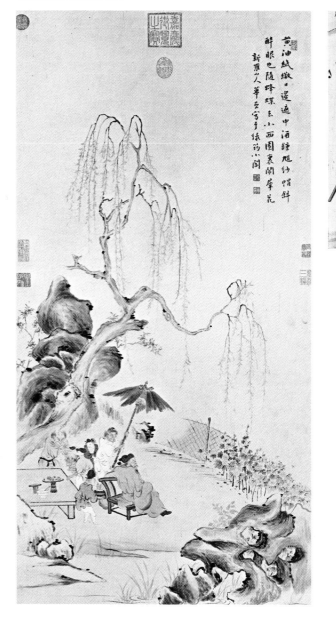

黃油紙緻以逅逺中酒鍾旭紗帽鮮
醉眼也隨蜂蝶玉小西園裏闌舉芫
新順久筆云寫于緒朌八闢

Science and technology did not fare well under the Ming. Up to this time the Chinese had been equal or superior to the Europeans in these areas. Their major inventions, such as printing and gunpowder, are well known. Other accomplishments are less generally acknowledged. The Chinese probably understood the principles of magnetism as early as A.D. 83, constructed the first iron bridge during the Sui dynasty, and invented a variety of useful machines by the Ming era, including a water-driven spinning wheel, a rotary fan for winnowing, and a silk-reeling machine run by treadle power. During the Ming dynasty, however, the advance of science was halted. No doubt there are many reasons for this ossification. The controlled marketplace, for example, discouraged individual entrepreneurs from using technological innovations to enhance productivity and profits. Prevailing attitudes among scholars and bureaucrats also contributed to the antiscientific malaise. "Ever since the time of the philosopher [the Neo-Confucian Chu Hsi]," wrote one Ming scholar, "the truth has

Above left, Chung K'uei in the Noonday Sun, *painted by Hua Yen in the eighteenth century. Chung K'uei, a gifted but physically repulsive scholar, won the right to receive his diploma from the emperor himself but was so mortified by the emperor's reaction to his appearance that he committed suicide. Top, a European cartographer's representation of two mandarins with a pair of phoenixes. Immediately above, a Chinese screen painter's depiction of a Portuguese ship and its crew.*

Above, the Great Wall, painted by an anonymous nineteenth-century European artist.

been made manifest to the world: No more writing is necessary. What is left to us is to practice." But the main reason for the lack of scientific and technological progress is that the best minds were directed toward passing the civil-service examinations. Talented Chinese wanted to become officials because this was the route to prestige and wealth. Technical skills, on the other hand, were popularly linked with commerce, which was officially disdained.

This antiscientific attitude took hold at a time when contacts with foreigners were more numerous than ever before. Chinese merchants actively traded in Southeast Asia, the East Indies, and Japan throughout his period. In the sixteenth century, Portuguese traders, however unwelcome, established themselves at Macao, just south of Canton, and in 1582 the Jesuit missionary Matteo Ricci received permission to take up residence inside the Middle Kingdom.

Ricci, a man of penetrating and disciplined intellect, was quick to impress Chinese officials with the value of Western science. Adopting the dress of a Confucian scholar, Ricci, assisted by his companion Michele Ruggieri, turned his chapel into a museum of European science, with clocks, drawings of European buildings, and glass prisms. Ricci's intellectual accomplishments—he produced, for example, a map of the world in a projection tactfully designed to give the Middle Kingdom a prominent central location—eventually brought him to the attention of Emperor Wan Li. The Jesuit soon became one of the emperor's favorites.

Matteo Ricci and his fellow missionaries made some converts, but on the whole there was little enthusiasm for the promises held out by a new, foreign religion. The Jesuits served the emperor as astronomers, interpreters, cartographers, painters, architects, and engineers—these turned out to be their principal functions in China.

Conditions in the provinces deteriorated steadily during the Ming dynasty, and in 1644 a peasant rebellion organized by one Li Tzu-ch'eng marched on Peking. The capital was virtually undefended, and

The Great Wall has often been rebuilt and extended. The portions of the wall most often visited today, especially those in the Peking foothills (these pages), were erected during the reign of the Ming emperor Wan Li (1572–1620).

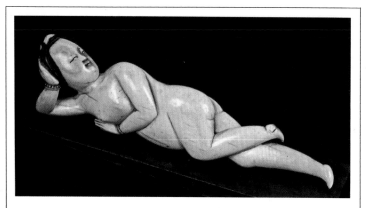

Medicine

Unlike Western medicine, which has traditionally isolated physical ailments and their causes, Chinese medicine has never separated the treatment of illness from philosophical—and even mystical—theories of health. Herbal cures and acupuncture, the treatments most often associated with oriental medicine today, were well established by Han times.

Although there is little evidence that popular remedies such as ginseng have any beneficial effect, the Chinese were superior botanists and knew of many herbal medicines of proven medical worth. Acupuncture, too, has been found to help those suffering from asthma, dermatitis, and other disorders, even though the theory—studied on models like the one illustrated below—cannot be proved in terms of Western medical knowledge. The Chinese even knew of a primitive vaccination for smallpox, which involved wearing a scab from a smallpox victim in one's nose, but the treatment of infectious diseases never fulfilled its early promise.

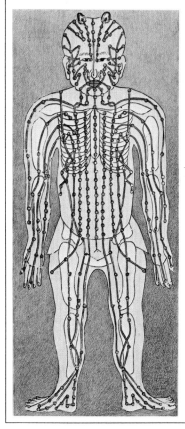

Above, a nude female figurine of the Ming dynasty. Physicians were usually not permitted to examine women; instead, the patient used the figurine to indicate the location of the pain.

This nineteenth-century anatomical diagram (left) illustrates the "meridians," or channels, that were thought to control the flow of body energies.

the Ming emperor, rather than fall into the hands of the insurgents, retired to a garden shed and hanged himself. The army, then stationed on the northern frontier, might have been able to rescue the dynasty, but its commander, Wu San-kuei, was so unnerved by stories of the rebel commander's cruelty that he lost all sense of prudence and sought assistance from the Manchu, whom he had been fighting.

The Manchu, a northern people related to the Ju-chen, were delighted by the prospect of an alliance with their former foe. Having previously been deterred from entering northern China as conquerors, they now entered Peking as allies of the imperial army—and there they stayed. A seven-year-old Manchu prince was proclaimed Son of Heaven, and China came under the domination of a new dynasty, the Ch'ing.

Although the Manchu were "barbarians," they had already assimilated a good deal of Chinese culture when the southern portion of Manchuria was under Ming rule. When they set up their government in Peking, they were prepared to preserve the Chinese bureaucracy, promote the study of the Confucian classics, and continue the old state cults. At the same time, they also sensed the dangers of becoming so assimilated that their national identity would be lost. For this reason, they forbade intermarriage between the Manchu and the Chinese and erected their own makeshift version of the Great Wall—a willow palisade with ditches on either side—to keep Chinese settlers out of the Manchu's ancestral homeland in northern Manchuria. In civil administration, the Manchu were content to allow Chinese officials to conduct business as usual, but they often designated a Manchu appointee to keep an eye on his Chinese colleagues.

The strengths of the Manchu dynasty at its height are seen in the rule of K'ang-hsi, who reigned from 1662 to 1722. K'ang-hsi's letters and edicts show him to have been a cultivated yet unpretentious man who was happiest when hunting in the Manchurian forests beyond the Great Wall. "There," he wrote, "are forests of oak and poplar and wild beech, and

Right, a Ch'ing dynasty landscape that expresses the continuing attraction of southern scenery as a subject for Chinese painters.

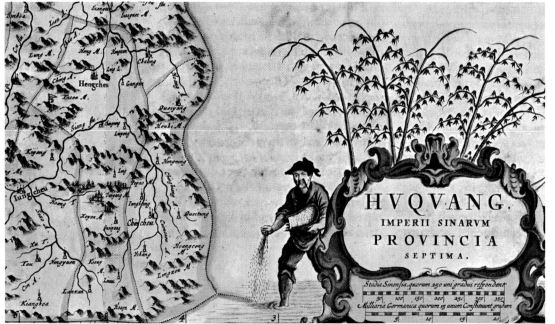

Rice

The southward migrations that began with the collapse of the Han dynasty led to a revolution in dietary habits. Tea, a drink unknown in Han times, was first adopted by southerners and gradually became popular with the upper classes in the north. Tang dynasty aristocrats also enjoyed such exotic tropical fruits as pineapples, bananas, and litchi nuts. But by far the most important of the new crops was rice. As early as A.D. 600, rice had become the staple food of the lower Yangtze Valley and southern coastal provinces. From the Sung dynasty on, new techniques were constantly being introduced to improve irrigation and increase productivity. Fish were sometimes stocked in flooded fields to provide food and at the same time control malaria-bearing mosquitoes. Botanists also developed fast-growing strains of rice that matured only sixty days after the seedlings were transplanted to the fields.

Right, The Rice Harvest, *painted during the T'ung-chih period of the Ch'ing dynasty (1862–1875).*

Above, utensils used in the preparation of rice. Left, rice mats hung up to dry.

Chinese potters sometimes pressed rice grains into unfired porcelain. The result was a design (such as on the plate below) that became visible only when the translucent china was held up to the light.

Navigation

Marco Polo, visiting the Middle Kingdom during the reign of the Yüan emperor Kublai Khan, compared the great trading city of Hangchow to his native Venice and noted admiringly that the volume of commerce on the Yangtze exceeded that of all of Europe's rivers put together. Among the public works sponsored by early emperors to encourage river traffic were the Grand Canal, a seven-hundred-mile link between north and south built under the Sui dynasty, and the Marine Wall, a one-hundred-and-eighty-mile-long dike that protected Yangtze boatmen from dangerous tidal bores.

Although Chinese vessels were relative latecomers to the high seas, they ranked among the finest in the world. Under the Ming emperor Yung Lo, an armada of sixty-two vessels sailed to India and expeditions were undertaken to Africa and to Aden on the Red Sea.

At the time of the Manchu invasion, Ming loyalists took to the seas off the southern coast. Cheng Ch'eng-kung, the son of one of these holdouts, became a fearsome pirate, raiding Chinese ports and terrorizing European traders, who knew him as Koxinga. Today, this "pirate-patriot" is best known for establishing Chinese control over the island of Formosa (Taiwan).

Left, the dial of a Chinese compass used during the eighteenth century. Below, a ceremonial boat belonging to a high official. The vessel is fitted out with banners and ornamental lanterns.

This three-masted junk (top) has been altered for travel on the open sea. Such vessels were used during the eighteenth century for military expeditions against Korea and Indonesia. Immediately above, a river boat for passenger transport.

Above and below, boats on the Li River. Until very recent times, Chinese families whose livelihoods depended on rivers often set up house on board their boats. There were entire houseboat cities whose residents seldom set foot on land.

Left, a junk under full sail on a lake in Szechwan Province.

Occupied by the British in 1841, Hong Kong (above) grew rapidly to a population of one hundred thousand Chinese and two thousand Europeans by 1893. The first Chinese ship (right) to round the Cape of Good Hope reached London in 1848 after 477 days at sea. Below, a tea sale attended by Chinese and Western merchants. The Chinese export-import trade was monopolized by an official guild, the Cohong.

wild pears and peaches, apples and apricots.... There is tea, made from fresh snow on the little brazier slung between two horses." And of course respite from the hot summers of Peking was also to be found. "You have to wear a fur jacket in the mornings," the emperor noted in one of his letters, "even though in Peking it is so hot that you hesitate about having the eunuchs lead the consorts out of the palaces to greet you on your return." For all of the delight he took in hunting, K'ang-hsi was also an extremely hard-working ruler. He successfully put down a rebellion by Wu San-kuei, applied himself to the problem of equalizing the tax burden, and even took a hand in an ar-

In 1842, Vice Admiral William Parker forced the Chinese to concede a small area along the Huang Pu River in Shanghai (above). This was the beginning of the transformation of the city into China's greatest commercial center. Foreigners lived in Western enclaves, exempt from Chinese laws.

gument between the Jesuit missionaries in China and their superiors back in Europe.

This argument, known as the Rites Controversy, was sparked by the Jesuits' politic accommodations to Chinese customs. Some of the practices the Jesuits tolerated were trivial, such as painting shoes on images of the crucified Christ because the Chinese were offended by bare feet. More significant, the Jesuits allowed their converts to continue observing the rituals of the Confucian cults, a duty expected of every Chinese subject. K'ang-hsi, who had previously convinced the Jesuit missionary Ferdinand Verbiest to produce 132 cannons for his campaign against Wu San-kuei, attempted to resolve the issue by declaring diplomatically to Vorbiest that the ritual homage the Chinese paid to Confucius and their ancestors was entirely secular. "We neither hope for nor expect anything from Confucius or the ancestors," he pro-

claimed. "What is read in the rituals that might suggest the contrary is no more than one of the many metaphors in the Chinese language." When this gracious compromise was rejected by the pope, K'ang-hsi was understandably disgusted but continued to treat the cooperative Jesuits at his court favorably. Some years after his death, however, the Rites Controversy led to his son's decision to denounce Christianity as subversive. Western science was rejected along with Western religion, and in 1747 an officially sponsored encyclopedia declared that Matteo Ricci's "description of the five continents is nothing more than a wild fabulous story."

In 1736, Ch'ien Lung, K'an-hsi's grandson, began a sixty-year reign that was to consolidate his grandfather's military gains in Mongolia, Tibet, and the southwestern province of Kweichow. During the early years of his reign, Ch'ien Lung tolerated Westerners, commissioning a Jesuit, for example, to paint portraits of the women of the imperial court. But in 1793, when a British embassy under Lord Macartney arrived in Peking seeking to open formal diplomatic relations, the emperor politely but firmly refused, declaring that there were well-established regulations governing envoys from foreign states to Peking. (China would never accept foreign envoys unless they came as bearers of tribute.) As for increasing the volume of trade with Britain, the emperor noted confidently that "the virtue and prestige of the Celestial dynasty having spread far and wide, the kings of the myriad nations come by land and sea with all sorts of precious things. Consequently, there is nothing we lack." Even Lord Macartney was forced to concede that this boast was not made entirely out of ignorance. Invited to tour the imperial summer palace, he was chagrined to discover whole pagodas filled with valuable gifts that put his embassy's own presents—which included two enameled watches and a pair of air guns—to shame.

If Lord Macartney had failed to make an impression on Ch'ien Lung, the Englishman returned the favor in his astute report on the mission. "The empire of China is an old, crazy, first-rate man of war, which a succession of able and vigilant officers has contrived to keep afloat these one hundred and fifty years past," he wrote. Sensing the vulnerability of the Manchu, England continued to fill its ships with low-bulk,

Left, English and French troops storming Canton during the Second Opium War of 1857. Canton, originally the only port open to Western merchants, had been the scene of the first attempt to halt the opium trade in 1839. It remained the busiest of the treaty ports.

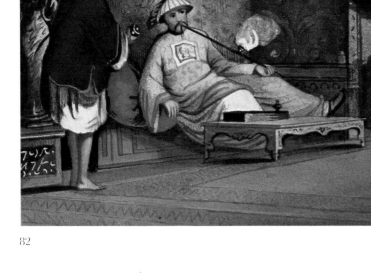

Left, opium smoking, as depicted in a mid-nineteenth-century engraving. Opium was known in China during Ming times, but its use did not become a prevalent social problem until the British began flooding the market in the 1800s. Both Chinese and foreign merchants made fortunes from the trade.

high-value opium. Chinese officials objected, but they were forced to capitulate as a result of the Opium War of 1839–1842.

One is tempted to blame the decline of the Ch'ing on the humiliating system of unequal treaties forced on China in the wake of the Opium Wars of 1839–1842 and of 1856–1860. But modern historians agree that the impact of Western imperialism only exacerbated other problems that had already begun to erode the stability of Chinese society. The greatest of these problems was China's exploding population. Under the Sung dynasty, China was inhabited by an estimated eighty million people. By 1741 the population had risen to about one hundred and forty-three million, and during the next century there was a still more dramatic increase—to over four hundred and fourteen million by 1850.

The pressures of so many additional people combined with Western encroachment to produce an overburdened bureaucracy and a restless, unstable peasantry. Peasant uprisings began as early as the mid-eighteenth century, but the most powerful and threatening insurgence was the Taiping Rebellion of one hundred years later. This rebellion was instigated by Hung Hsiu-ch'üan, a poor man from a despised ethnic minority group who had three times failed the imperial examinations. The movement Hung founded included many Christian elements and was anti-Confucian, advocating communal ownership of property, equal rights for women, and a repudiation of foreign treaties signed by the Manchu. In 1853 the Taiping, who numbered in the hundreds of thousands, seized Nanking, one of the most important cities of southern China. But Hung had no notion of how to turn his success into a lasting government; he eventually went mad and was unable to take an active role in the rebellion. While Hung busied himself with his eighty-eight wives—accumulated in spite of his own preaching of monogamy—his generals fell to squabbling among themselves, and by 1864, Nanking was back in Manchu hands.

Caught between peasant rebellions and the increasingly aggressive demands of the European powers, the Chinese were at last forced to debate the

On May 20, 1858, French and English troops attacked the Taku forts (below), China's line of defense between the Strait of Pohai and Peking. The Ch'ing army, equipped with only a few outmoded cannons and already weakened by the Taiping Rebellion, quickly collapsed.

merits of westernization. The example of a modernizing Japan could not be ignored, especially after 1895, when the poorly organized Chinese army suffered a crushing defeat in a Sino-Japanese war over control of Korea. The Japanese seized the Manchurian city of Port Arthur (Lüshun) and began a campaign for possession of the Manchu homeland that was to persist into the twentieth century. Worse still, China was forced to borrow from European bankers to pay an indemnity to the Japanese, and its weakened position touched off a further scramble for territorial concessions.

In spite of these alarming developments, many educated Chinese still worried less about outright conquest than about the destruction of their cultural heritage by foreign ideas. The Middle Kingdom had been conquered before and survived, but voluntary abandonment of Confucian values was unthinkable. After the defeat by Japan, societies calling for national "self-strengthening" sprang up throughout China. However, the most influential of these reformers still hoped that it would be possible to pick and choose the elements of European culture that suited Chinese needs, believing that European and Chinese cultures could still be reconciled. Even K'ang Yu-wei, a scholar who advocated the establishment of a constitutional government, did so through a study

called *Confucius the Reformer,* which described the revered sage as an advocate of progress and a believer in the power of the people to check authoritarian rule.

By 1898, K'ang Yu-wei gained the ear of the sickly young man who had the ill luck to be the occupant of the Dragon Throne at the time. Day after day, the emperor was told of China's weakness as compared to Europe until, at last, he agreed in despair that "Westerners all pursue useful studies, while we Chinese pursue useless studies. Thus the present situation is brought about." The emperor's attempt to change this state of affairs was dramatic. In a flurry of edicts, he ordered the first government bond issue in an attempt to repay China's foreign debts, called for the establishment of trade schools, set up a bureau of mines and railroads, and commanded journalists to write about political affairs. But the emperor's most controversial move was the abolition of the "eight-legged essay" in the civil-service examinations: The emphasis in the exams was now to be placed on mastery of practical skills, not just the art of composition.

The leaders of this so-called Hundred Days of Reform had not counted on the power of the dowager empress Tz'u Hsi. A former imperial concubine, Tz'u Hsi had already guided China through two regencies, ruling first in the name of her son and later in the name of her nephew, the emperor at the time of the

Peking was surrounded by a fortified wall built during the Mongol, or Yüan, dynasty. The Fucheng gate (left) opened onto the goat market and the saddlers' quarter. Gate towers up to 161 feet tall served as armories and troop billets.

Right, the dowager empress Tz'u Hsi, in a painting copied from a photograph by an anonymous Chinese artist.

Left, the execution of a Boxer leader. Above, a nineteenth-century German lithograph showing Western armies massing outside the Great Wall as a furious but impotent China makes threatening gestures. The original caption read: "Greetings from the Great Wall of China."

reforms. Tz'u Hsi now became a rallying point for disaffected conservatives. When overconfident reformers sounded out the popular general Yüan Shih-k'ai on the possibility of a coup against the dowager empress and her favorites, the general promptly informed the dowager empress' loyal servants of the plot. Now sixty-three years old, Tz'u Hsi had successfully manipulated court politics for thirty-eight years and was not to be so easily dislodged. On the morning of September 22, 1898, she swept into the young emperor's apartments and accused him of filial disloyalty. On her instructions, the hapless Son of Heaven was taken away to an island palace outside the walls of Peking's Forbidden City, where he remained a virtual prisoner. Some of the reformers fled, six were executed, and the decrees of the Hundred Days were rescinded.

Tz'u Hsi without question possessed the qualities of leadership that her idealistic nephew so sorely lacked. Having lived within the walls of the Forbidden City since the age of sixteen, however, she had little knowledge of the outside world and no loyalties except to the court eunuchs and a few relatives and officials who had supported her in the past. Her limited grasp of foreign affairs was demonstrated by the way she handled the uprising that confronted China in the spring of 1900—the Boxer Rebellion.

The Boxer Rebellion takes its name from the term foreigners used to designate the members of the secret society known as the Righteous and Harmonious Fists. The Boxer insurgents, who practiced boxing and calisthenic rituals in the belief that they would become impervious to bullets, did not seek the overthrow of the Ch'ing dynasty. Their targets instead were missionaries, who were accused of using the intestines and eyes of Chinese orphans to brew medicines, and foreign businessmen, whose railroads were said to have disturbed the peace of the "terrestrial dragon" by passing over or near sacred ground. T'zu Hsi and her entourage apparently thought that they could use the Boxers to humiliate the foreign community and therefore encouraged the rebels. In the summer of 1900 the Boxers reached Peking, where

During the Boxer Rebellion of 1900, European residents of Peking were besieged for fifty-five days inside the Legation Quarter (left) until the arrival of a relief expedition (above) composed of troops from seven Western nations and Japan. Thousands of Chinese Christians lost their lives during the insurgence, but one member of the relief force noted that the European ladies "looked as if they had stepped out of a band-box."

Right, executions following the suppression of the rebels. The reparations imposed on China in the wake of the rebellion were the final blow to Manchu sovereignty.

they besieged the foreign legations for sixty days. Some European diplomats and missionaries were killed, but the majority of the Boxers' victims were Chinese Christians, who died by the thousands. On August 14, a British relief expedition reached Peking and liberated the legations. When a stray bullet flew through the window of Tz'u Hsi's private quarters, the dowager empress suddenly remembered that she had been planning an "inspection tour" of Manchuria. Dressing herself as a peasant woman, she ordered the emperor and his appointed heir into horse-drawn carts and set off hastily for the north.

Peking was now conquered, but its new rulers were totally unprepared to govern all of China. Eventually, having no one else to put on the Dragon Throne, the foreign powers invited Tz'u Hsi to return to the capital. The dowager empress, much chastened by her last-minute flight, was at last ready to listen to the reformers. But the Heaven's mandate had run out for the Ch'ing dynasty. In payment for what were exaggeratedly described as "crimes unprecedented in human history," the Chinese were ordered to pay a reparation of sixty-seven million pounds sterling. On top of an already ruinous foreign debt, this left little to finance meaningful reforms. In addition, the landlord and gentry families of the provinces were by no means eager to see the rise of a strongly centralized, pro-Western imperial bureaucracy. The tide was turning in favor of a new movement among Western-educated Chinese, one that favored revolution over mere reform.

The elderly Tz'u Hsi died in November of 1908. Her nephew, the emperor, predeceased her by one day, perhaps poisoned by the courtiers who had tormented him for so long and now feared his impending revenge. Tz'u Hsi's chosen heir, a two-year-old princeling, assumed the imperial throne, but a wave of anti-Manchu feeling swept the country and the child-emperor's regents abdicated in 1912; in their final statements, the regents noted that "the people's wishes are plain." Although the revolutionary theorist Sun Yat-sen had already been declared president of the new republic, it was agreed that Yüan Shih-k'ai—the most powerful man in China—was to take over formally after the Manchu abdication.

Yüan Shih-k'ai attempted to use his position to found a dynasty. In 1915, having already dismissed China's first legally elected parliament, Yüan declared himself emperor, the first of a new Han dynasty. The foreign powers, who viewed Yüan as a stabilizing force, expressed guarded approval, but the indignation that swept throughout China demonstrated that the imperial ideal was obsolete. Yüan died of natural causes before he could be deposed. The former emperor, meanwhile, survived to become a puppet of the Japanese occupation forces in Manchuria in the 1930s and 1940s and, eventually, a clerk in the People's Republic of China, where he died in 1967.

Islands of the Rising Sun

According to the Japanese myth of creation, the divine origins of both the land and its emperors can be traced to the god Izanagi and his consort-sister, Izanami. Tales reveal that the happy pair were out on a celestial fishing expedition one day, deftly plucking their catch from the heavenly sea with a jeweled spear, when lo and behold, drops falling from the spear chanced to fall to earth. Magically, they took shape as Japan, an archipelago of countless islands, towering mountains, and verdant plains.

Delighted with what they had done, Izanagi promptly celebrated their feat by giving birth through his left eye to Amaterasu, the sun goddess, and through his right eye to Tsukiyomi, the god of

the moon. As time passed, still more divine children were produced by the heavenly host, climaxing in the birth of Susanō, the god of fire, storms, and destruction. Amaterasu and Susanō grew up to become sworn enemies, and their offspring, assuming the rivalry, entered into perpetual warfare with one another.

When heaven could no longer contain the conflict, the warring clan-factions carried the battle to earth. Ninigi-no-Mikoto, grandson of Amaterasu, and consequently chief of the Tenson, or Sun Line, settled in Kyūshū, southernmost of the four large islands of Japan. With him he brought the Three Treasures—a bronze mirror, a curved jewel, and an iron sword— that had been given to him by his grandmother. These regalia, symbols representing the sun, the moon, and lightning, proved to be divine talismen, for Ninigi's descendants were able to fight their way north until they had conquered the stronghold of Susanō's descendants (a clan that had taken the name of the Izumo) on the north coast of western Honshū, another of Japan's main islands.

The victors then turned east to the opposite coast, subduing the descendant clans of still other fractious gods and establishing a formal seat of government in the Yamato region. The myth concludes triumphantly with Ninigi's grandson being recognized by his retinue as Jimmu Tenno, divine warrior and emperor of heaven, in the legendary year 660 B.C.

Appealing as this tale of creation is, a more illuminating approach to Japan's origins, physical as well as human, might better begin with a description of its actual geography. Japan is a curving chain of four large islands—Kyūshū, Shikoku, Honshū, and Hokkaidō—and nearly a thousand smaller islands, created by volcanic eruptions of the earth's crust. The archipelago stretches for a thousand miles on roughly

Rising out of the sea, a torii *(ca. A.D. 600), or gate (preceding page), leads to the ancient Shinto site of Itsukushima, on an island in Hiroshima Bay.*

Near right, the southeast coast of the island of Tōchi as seen from Mount Washiji. Far right, top to bottom, the craggy elevations of Karasawa, in the Japanese Alps, central Honshū; Mount Aso, an active volcano on Kyūshū, boasting a crater fifteen miles in diameter; and Towada-ko, a vast lake occupying a volcanic depression in the Nasu volcanic zone of northernmost Honshū.

a southwest to northeast arc off the coast of the east Asian mainland between twenty-four degrees and forty-six degrees north latitude. Japan's total land size, some 142,000 square miles, makes it slightly smaller than California but slightly larger than the British Isles. Unlike either of these places, however, only a small part of the territory is arable. As a result, the Japanese people have had to cluster on the few small pockets of flat land, most of them riverine plains formed along the coastlines at the termini of short, swift-flowing rivers.

The country's human history, as far as archaeologists have been able to determine from Paleolithic tools, most probably began between ten thousand and thirty thousand years ago. It remains a mystery who the first settlers were, but they are presumed to have been hunters and gatherers who arrived from the Asian continent by way of the land bridge that once existed between Korea and Honshū across the 120-mile-wide Korea Strait. Based on similarities noted in the Japanese Paleolithic artifacts and those

found in Mongolia, Manchuria, and Korea, anthropologists conclude further that the first inhabitants of Japan were of Caucasic stock. Indeed, the language spoken in modern Japan is grouped with the Altaic tongues, whose first speakers have been traced to central Asia and the Altai Mountains.

A less numerous but significant southern strain, made up of peoples from Southeast Asia and from the southern and eastern coastal regions of China, arrived somewhat later. Still another ancient tribal group were the Ainu, primitive Caucasians perhaps related to the Caucasoids of northern Siberia, whose numbers were few and whose technological culture, inferior to that of other groups, caused them over the centuries to retreat for survival ever deeper into the most remote parts of Japan until they occupied only small portions of the island of Hokkaidō. Their markedly different appearance distinguished them from the rest of the Japanese stock: They had fair skin, lighter and more plentiful hair than is common to other Japanese, and eyes that had the Mongolian fold. Speaking

Much of the Japanese landscape has shown little change over the centuries. Left, autumn on picturesque Lake Yago. Immediately below, rice fields in central Honshū. Paddy fields, the major type of rice field in Japan, are found in every part of the country, evident on hillsides as well as on plains; over half of all cultivated land produces rice. The wet method of rice cultivation, introduced ca. 250 B.C. by migrants from the Asian mainland, gave rise to an intricate system of *watercourses, watergates, ditches, dikes, and ponds to provide proper irrigation and to prevent flooding. Throughout most of Japan, the land yields two or three harvests a year. Seldom allowed to lie fallow, the fields are seeded for wheat, rushes, rapeseed, and many other crops in the winter when rice is not cultivated. Bottom, typical Japanese dwellings and fruit fields in Azu-no-Sato, an apricot-producing village in the prefecture of Magano.*

a language of their own, they remained isolated from the rest of their countrymen from the beginning. To this day they survive in tiny enclaves apart from others.

The first major cultural group, characterized by the development of pottery making and preceding that of farming, dates from the fifth or fourth millennium. Called the Jōmon after the *jōmon,* or cord marks, that decorated much of the hand-shaped pottery, they appear to be Neolithic people of considerable sophistication. Evidence from the several hundred archaeological sites so far discovered reveals that the Jōmon were distributed in small tribal groups over the habitable portions of the Japanese archipelago, with certain regional differences developing as centers of the culture matured. Gradually the Jōmon melded with the earlier Mongoloid peoples into a homogeneous population.

Beginning around 300 B.C., the Jōmon were gradually displaced and once again absorbed by a Neolithic people known to modern scholars as the Yayoi, a name

The Neolithic Jōmon culture, characterized by the custom of using jōmon, or twisted cord, to impress designs into the wet clay before firing, has produced impressive clay artifacts. This dogū (left), or clay figure, dates from the fourth to third century B.C. This standing effigy (right), from a somewhat later date, shows a more elaborate decoration, including indications of a necklace and a costume with swirl motifs. Both figures are believed to be representations of gods of the Jōmon culture. This terracotta vase (below right) of the Middle Jōmon period was given its surface texture by pressing a combination of woven matting and cord into the material. Some seventy different shapes of pottery have been found in Jōmon tombs.

taken from the district in modern Tokyo where, in A.D. 1884, the first pottery artifacts of this group were excavated. Though detailed information on the origins of the Yayoi is still lacking, the most conclusive evidence suggests that they were of Mongoloid stock with traditions that tied them culturally and probably racially to the nomadic tribes of central Asia. Their movement into Japan, and into Korea before that, was probably the result of the growing strength of China. China already consisted of a unified state with an organized system of government administration, a military caste, and advanced technology comprising skills in making iron tools, in canal building, in irrigation for farming, and in writing. Gradually the Chinese had driven their less powerful neighbors to seek refuge in the south of Korea, sending the Yayoi on their way with small bits of new knowledge that advanced the cultural groups with whom they were to come in contact.

The Yayoi were technologically, if not always artistically, superior to the Jōmon. Most notably, the Yayoi were farmers, practicing the wet cultivation of rice, including the construction of paddy fields, irrigation channels, dams, and other cooperative waterworks that tended to give coherence to their communities. Their pottery, while typically less ornate and more utilitarian, was wheel turned (Jōmon pottery was hand formed) and was fired at higher temperatures that made for finer, more durable ware. They carried with them numerous Chinese-made objects, especially small ritual bronzes such as bells and ceremonial weapons, and they appear to have kept alive cultural contacts with China and with those parts of Korea where colonies of Chinese had settled. It was in their new homeland of Japan, however, that the Yayoi learned to cast bronze.

Sometime around A.D. 250, a new Bronze Age society, based on the Kofun, or Tomb, culture, began to have an impact on Yayoi Japan. Scholars disagree as to whether the people of the Kofun culture represented a new wave of Mongolian immigrants or simply an indigenous development of mature Yayoi people, influenced perhaps by contact with the mainland. In either case, a warrior class—men who fought on horseback, wore armor, and wielded long, straight iron swords—became the dominant force in the land. Soon they constituted an established aristocracy, whose initial authority was secured by force but whose continued strength was derived from clan membership and prestige. They dominated a society that willingly paid tribute in return for protection.

Among the most striking evidence of this major change are the massive burial mounds that first appeared in the Kansai plain, a five-hundred-square-mile-area on west-central Honshū, where the principal Kofun culture settlements lay. The earlier Yayoi had buried the dead of every rank in clay urns or stone coffins set in the earth with scarcely a device to mark them for posterity. The Kofun people, however, built huge earthworks for their leaders, indicating a quantum leap in political power and organization.

A shadowy image of the Tomb people has been pieced together from a wealth of tools, jewelry, and pottery figurines called *haniwa*, buried in the mounds, as well as from ancient chronicles of the Chinese who, even before the dawn of the Christian era, began to

make trade contacts with their neighbors. These accounts suggest that ritual dancing played an important part in life, that body designs and differences of clothing had already developed to indicate rank, and that a religion based on nature and ancestor worship had taken hold, the forerunner of Japan's national cult of Shinto.

In this hierarchical society, three groups—the *uji, be,* and *yatsuko*—typically made up each community or state. The uji leaders functioned as the aristocracy, responsible for government, warfare, and religious affairs, including supplicating the gods. Nominally, all members of the uji claimed descent from a common god-ancestor, usually a figure associated with a natural phenomenon, like the sun, moon, lightning, fertility, and the like; all within a uji recognized among their earthly living members a *uji-no-kami,* or clan chief, who was regarded as first among equals and venerated as semidivine. From an early date, occupational specialization appears to have developed among the uji. For example, certain warrior clans, such as the Mononobe, produced military men, though in each case the states over which they presided remained chiefly agricultural.

Beneath the uji elite and bound in service to them were a large and diverse class of be, or workers. The

Haniwas, *or funerary statuettes, such as those shown here, were the handiwork of the Yayoi, Neolithic people who first appeared in Japan ca. 300 B.C. This powerful visage (left) represents a monkey's head. Right, a figure with an open mouth—perhaps a priest chanting a hymn. Below, a detail from a realistically modeled seated figure, suggesting in its exaggerated headdress and jewelry northern Asiatic dress. Haniwas were typically arranged in concentric circles in the ground around the burial mounds of Yayoi priest-kings—as ornamentation, as a means of stabilizing the loose earth, and sometimes to ward off evil spirits.*

Mount Fuji

In a nation imbued with a deep reverence for nature, Mount Fuji is among the most sacred of the islands' natural wonders. It is held to be the dwelling place of a *kami*, or spirit, named Kono-hana-sakuyahime-no-mikoto, the consort of Ninigi. As Ninigi was the grandson of the sun goddess and an ancestor of the first earthly emperor, Fuji is regarded as a living representation of the nation's divine origins. A number of shrines are erected on its slopes, and for centuries pilgrims have thronged there to pay homage. Fuji plays a role in numerous myths, one being "The Tale of the Bamboo Cutter." In this legend the Shining Princess gives the emperor *Fushi no kusuri*, the Elixir of Life, which he orders to be sprinkled over the great volcano's cone. Eventually, Fushi may have come to be pronounced Fuji, whence came the mountain's name. Another theory holds that Fuji derives from the Ainu word for "fire."

Mount Fuji in southcentral Honshū towers over Kawaguchi (right), one of several communities settled along the fertile plains that fan out from its broad base. Among the youngest of Japan's five hundred volcanos, Mount Fuji is 12,389 feet in altitude, with a roughly circular crater at its summit that is some two thousand feet in diameter. On a clear day the peak is visible as far away as Tokyo, fifty-five miles to the southwest. Below and on preceding pages, two of the five volcanic lakes formed on the north and northeast sides of Fuji. The area's notable tranquility was last disrupted in 1707 when Fuji rained molten lava and ashes down on the surrounding land.

Right, The Great Wave near the Coast of Kanagawa, *by Katsushika Hokusai. This turbulent seascape was part of a series of woodblock prints entitled* Thirty-six Views of Fuji, *published in 1820. Hokusai, who described himself as* "The Old Man Mad with Painting," *undertook some one hundred and fifty depictions of the holy mountain during his eighty-nine years in an attempt to capture its great beauty and mystery. Kanagawa, located near Yokohama, was briefly offered as an open port when Commodore Perry established America's first trading contacts with Japan some three and a half decades after Hokusai visited there.*

Left, Ando Hiroshige's nineteenth-century woodblock entitled Amaterasu on Fuji. *Though Amaterasu, the sun goddess, is not specifically associated with the creation of Fuji—one legend has it that an earthquake in 286 B.C. was responsible—she is believed to cast her protective mantle over all things sacred to Japanese life. Above, still another view of Fuji by an anonymous artist.*

Right, another view of the Hōryūji complex. To the left of the pagoda is the kondō, or Golden Hall, probably the oldest wooden building extant in the world. The kondō serves as a repository for temple paintings and statues. Not shown, but typical of such complexes, is a prominent chūmon, or middle gate. The chūmon at Hōryūji is guarded by one of the Niō twins (below).

This one-hundred-foot-high wooden pagoda (above) is part of the ancient Buddhist complex of Hōryūji near Nara, Japan's first formal capital, established in A.D. 704. Built in 607 by Prince Shōtoku, a devout Buddhist and imperial regent, the pagoda symbolizes the soaring spiritual aspirations of faith.

majority of them were farmers, though many were weavers, metal workers, and soldiers. Their positions within the community were frozen by hereditary tradition: The sons of weavers became weavers, and so on. Though only partially related by blood kinship, the members of a be recognized a single headman for their group as well as the uji overlords they served.

At the bottom of the social structure were the yatsuko, the slaves, who were a small minority relegated to domestic service in uji households. Most yatsuko were former be who had been taken captive in battle or were the descendants of such unfortunates. Skilled foreigners, who found their way to Japan through commerce of some other peaceful contact and chose

to stay, were typically absorbed into the be class.

Sometime around the middle of the fourth century A.D., the Yamato uji, who lived on the same Kansai plain that had seen the rise of the Kofun people, emerged from the welter of small, similarly constructed states. Yamato was naturally well situated for such a unifying role, with its territory central to other Japanese settlements and its low-lying land among the most productive for wet rice cultivation.

The Yamato uji also had the foresight to claim direct descent from the sun goddess, Amaterasu, a debatable lineage which they shrewdly legitimized by invoking Japan's ancient creation myth. To prove this claim, the uji-no-kami of Yamato could even produce the Three Treasures that Amaterasu had given his ancestor so many ages before. (The same Three Treasures remain a part of the Japanese imperial regalia to this day.)

With Japan's uji unified under Yamato leadership, the new emperor launched a series of military adventures on the Korean peninsula. This action won the grudging friendship of the kingdom of Paikche, which commenced sending tribute and craftsmen skilled in Chinese arts and technology. The Japanese summarily subdued the kingdom of Kaya, or Mimana, south of Paikche, and made it a virtual exten-

Right, the head of the Great Buddha (Dai-butsu) in the Tōdai-ji, or Great Eastern Temple, at Nara. Begun in 735, this figure, which rises some fifty feet above its lotus throne, took fourteen years to complete. It represents the Roshana Buddha, that incarnation which the Japanese identified with their Shinto sun goddess. Below, a detail of a Fetiche Buddha, located to the right of the main gate of the Tōdai-ji.

sion of Japanese territory, complete with a military governor.

With trade and communication thus greatly increased, the Yamato court soon found it was badly in need of scribes and other learned men to keep track of business, send and receive messages, and set down the annals of the court's successes. Sometime before A.D. 391, the court requested from the ruler of Paikche a man skilled in reading and writing Chinese characters (the lingua franca of eastern Asia) to be included in the next embassy. A scribe named Wani soon appeared in Yamato, and it is believed that he was set to work teaching his mysterious art to the imperial prince and to a few select young members of the aristocracy. Another theory suggests that there may have been a number of Korean and Chinese scribes imported to undertake these difficult and meticulous chores. In either case, the Chinese written language took its place alongside spoken Japanese as the official communication of the imperial court; as a result, government proclamations, genealogical records, written exchanges between the emperor and provincial leaders, and other devices crucial to the enhancement of imperial authority became a part of government function. Equally important for the history of Japan, the adoption of the Chinese written

language prepared the ground for the importation of Chinese culture, Confucian philosophy, and Buddhist religion—enrichments that would ultimately transform Japan from its still crude state into a major Asian civilization.

The traditional date for the introduction of Buddhism from China is said to be A.D. 552. As related in the *Nihon Shoki,* or the *History of Japan,* one of the main Japanese sources of ancient history compiled from oral records in the early eighth century, the king of Paikche was indirectly responsible for introducing Buddhism. Finding himself under ever increasing attack from armies of neighboring Silla, he sent a succession of ministers to the Yamato court in the first half of the sixth century, imploring the emperor to lend military protection. As the requests grew more urgent, the tributes also increased, and in 552 the Korean ruler dispatched a bronze image of Buddha together with a number of volumes of the *sutras,* or holy scriptures, and a letter praising Buddhism. Enlightenment had come to Paikche from China long before, wrote the king, and those who embraced its teachings would ultimately realize all their desires. When no help was forthcoming from the Japanese, the king sent a number of Buddhist monks together with men learned in Chinese medicine, the art of

The Great Hall of the Daibutsu (above) is a massive structure, 284 feet long, 166 feet wide, and 152 feet high. It is also distinguished by the fine detailing on its roofs. Left, masu-gumi, brackets that support the broadly overhanging eaves, and below, a shibi, or gilded crook-shaped finial, intended to ward off fire.

divination, calendar making, and classical Chinese texts.

The gifts caused considerable consternation in court. Not only did the most powerful clans disagree on rendering help to Paikche, they disagreed on the desirability of adopting Buddhism. The Japanese already had a native religion that served them well: By now their polytheistic nature worship had developed enough to have a name, Shinto, or Way of the Gods, and a number of formalized practices over which the emperor presided as high priest. And yet it was evident to many Japanese aristocrats, as it had been to the Koreans, that the Chinese, who worshiped Buddha, had a civilization far more stable, more advanced, and wealthier in material goods than their own.

The Yamato emperor was unable to make a decision on either the political or the religious issue and he turned to his counselors for guidance. The majority, whose power was legitimized by its asserted descent from a host of Shinto deities, was firmly opposed to the new faith and to further involvement with the mainland whence came such dangerous notions. But Iname, the chieftain of a clan called the Soga and only recently elevated to the inner circles of power, had little to lose by championing Buddhism and a great deal to gain if he won adherents; he therefore urged the emperor to embrace the new religion. The emperor declined after weighing the matter but he gave permission to the Soga to experiment with Buddhism on their own and turned over to them the Korean Buddha and the sutras for study.

For more than thirty years, the Soga clan quietly promoted itself and Buddhism while the Yamato emperor struggled unsuccessfully to keep Japan's foothold in Korea and to hold his fractious ujis together. In 562 the kingdom of Silla displaced the Japanese in Mimana, and in 587 problems at court culminated in open warfare between the Soga and a uji of hereditary generals, the Mononobe.

The victorious Soga, their power and prestige greatly enhanced, now felt safe to operate without the

Among the major figures responsible for spreading Buddhism to Japan were the seventh-century Chinese missionary Jion Daishi (above far left) and Prince Shōtoku Taishi, shown here with his two sons (above left). Left, the death of Gautama Buddha (attended by the bodhisattvas, or "Buddhas-elect") on his journey to Nirvana. Right, a seventeenth-century bronze effigy of Miroku, Buddha's successor, due to appear on earth 5,670 million years after Buddha's arrival in Nirvana to lead the faithful to salvation.

approval of the Yamato counselors. They channeled the Mononobe wealth directly into the building of Buddhist temples and monasteries and into the enlargement of the clergy. Five years later, Soga-no-Umako, son and successor of Iname and by now the top-ranking counselor of state, overcame the last major obstacle to Soga ascendancy by arranging for the assassination of the emperor Sujun and replacing him with a female member of the Sun Line, the thirty-nine-year-old Princess Suiko. Soga-no-Umako then named as regent and heir apparent Prince Shōtoku Taishi, Suiko's nephew and a devout Buddhist intellectual.

Shōtoku proved to be one of the great figures in Japanese history. He was both an effective conveyor of Chinese culture to the Japanese and a creative leader able to invest the throne with a measure of authority and dignity that had been lacking. Before

his death, Buddhism had become the official state religion and a code, based on Buddhist and Confucian ethics, was set forth for the management of government.

In a constitution attributed to Shōtoku, and most certainly summarizing his beliefs, the emperor declared: "Harmony is to be valued, and avoidance of wanton opposition to be honored." Sixteen other articles extolled such typically Confucian virtues as humanism, rationalism, and the obligation of the ruler to rule for the welfare of his subjects.

Shōtoku's code was not able to transform the uji into a bureaucracy of merit or his new office into an absolute monarchy (which together ran China), but he made a start, establishing twelve court ranks and giving each a distinctively colored cap as a means of rank identification. (In China such ranking depended on rigorous competitive examinations; in Japan rank

Here, scenes from the five-year battle (1180–1185) between the Minamoto and Taira. Above, the armies of Minamoto no Yorimasa preparing to charge against the forces of Taira no Kiyomori in 1180 at the River Uji. Ishida no Jiro of the Taira league (below) is shown before launching the fatal arrow against Minamoto no Yoshinaka at Awazu in 1184. Right, birds flying up to terrify the Taira. Left, the naval battle at Dannoura in 1185, in which the Taira fleet was sunk. Minamoto warriors storm the palace at Fukuhara (following pages).

In this tableau (left), a seated Minamoto no Yoshitsune reads orders to the warrior-monk Benkei. Yoshitsune was responsible for his league's military victories, but his elder brother Yoritomo (below), in somber robes and holding a shaku (a tablet indicating his exalted status), became clan leader and the most powerful man in Japan. Above, Yoritomo being received by the emperor in Kyōto in 1192.

continued to be influenced by hereditary privileges, effectively stifling excellence among governors.)

Of more far-reaching importance was Shōtoku's inauguration of the first of a series of official missions to the Chinese court for the purpose of establishing diplomatic and cultural ties. He directed scores of Japan's most promising young aristocrats to accompany the missions to study at first hand Chinese art, poetry, philosophy, government, history, science, Buddhist theology, and other gifts of the Tang dynasty (618–907). Reflecting Shōtoku's new sense of destiny for Japan, his emissaries were instructed to go not as supplicants, as their ancestors had occasionally done, but as representatives of a court that judged itself a substantial power. The self-styled "Emperor of the Rising Sun" even dared to address the Tang dynasty leader in an introductory letter as the "Emperor of the Setting Sun," a touch of humor that must have come dangerously close to offending the Chinese host.

Prince Shōtoku died in 621 before many of his reforms had time to take effect. The Soga family, unprepared for the independence of its hand-picked regent and emperor and sharing none of his idealism, made a series of moves to re-establish control of the imperial throne and even to usurp some of its prerogatives for its own members.

When political routes to their ambitions were thwarted, the Soga resorted to assassination once again, this time exterminating Shōtoku's heir and all of his family. But it was too late to reverse the trend that Shōtoku had begun. The very men whom he had sent to China in their youth were now established men of position and influence in Japan who wanted no less than a total reform of government along Chinese models.

Eventually, the leader of the Nakatomi uji, a clan composed of the hereditary chief priests of the Shinto faith, gathered support for a coup d'état. Nakatomi no Kamatari, aided by one of the imperial princes, murdered the head of the Soga in 645, forced the abdication of the Soga-appointed empress, and elevated Prince Kōtoku, another member of the Sun Line uji, to the throne.

The new leader, under the guidance of the Nakatomi (who henceforth assumed the surname of Fujiwara), set about to turn Shōtoku's idealized theories of state into practical realities with the Fujiwara as major beneficiaries. In a matter of months, Kōtoku called together the heads of the most important uji and announced sweeping administrative changes, among them a series of edicts that would come to be known as the Taika Reforms, or "Great Transforma-

Harvesting the sea

Surrounded by seas abundant in fish and lacking suitable land for raising livestock, the Japanese have made fishing a mainstay of their economy and fish a staple of their diet since ancient times. The growth of the fishing industry was also encouraged by the Buddhist prohibition against killing animals, which gave the Orthodox Japanese little choice about the type of protein they could consume. *Sashimi,* or sliced fish eaten raw, was a special favorite, a delicacy that was within the reach of the many Japanese who lived within a few miles of the sea. As freshness was the objective in preparing such a dish, the sashimi master would soak his slicing knife in water for several hours before cutting a fish, lest any trace of the flavor of the whetstone sully the delicate flesh.

Japanese attitudes toward fish relaxed in the latter half of the nineteenth century, when some proponents of modernization advanced the theory that eating red meat might be the chief reason for the Europeans' superior technical culture. After that, Japan's singular dependence on fish gave way to a mixed diet, and beef eating became a symbol of the avante-garde. The emperor officially added beef to his diet in 1872, and the *batakusai* (alien, exotic) carnivores felt free to practice their once-offensive eating habits in public. The majority of Japanese, however, continued to eat and enjoy their fish.

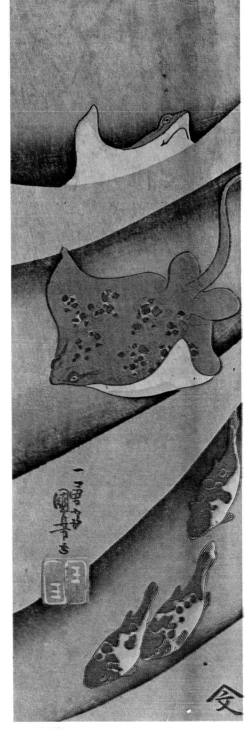

Below left, a small fishing boat of traditional design. Typically, such vessels are used as draggers, their large nets being towed astern as the skipper, tacking off the wind, uses his oversized gaff-rigged sail to propel the rig. Left, Fish, *by Utagawa Kuniyoshi, ca. 1840. Two panther rays glide by languorously while three* fugu, *globe fish, dart downward. Both are caught as food.*

Above, Japanese whalers in the North Pacific, in this print by Utagawa Kuniyoshi (ca. 1860). A typical pursuit fleet consisted of twenty "beater" boats and six "net" boats. When a whale was sighted, the beater boats (in the background) would surround the whale, their crews beating on the sides of their small vessels to drive their quarry toward the net boats where capture and kill were completed. In the foreground, workers are seen stripping blubber from whales already beached.

Tuna fishing is the subject of this eighteenth-century painting (left). Fishermen hunted the tuna, a large and lively game fish, with harpoons, in organized tuna fishing grounds. The fish played a large part in the Japanese diet, and still does today.

Immediately above, a mid-nineteenth-century print by Utagawa Kuniyoshi showing ama, or young women divers, gathering abalone, a shellfish prized both for its edibility and for the mother of pearl that lines its shell. In more recent times, ama have been used in commercial pearl production in Japan; their task is to collect young oysters that are subsequently implanted with a nacreous core around which a pearl obligingly forms. The oysters are then placed in cages and returned to the water for several years of cultivation.

The art of the silk weaver

Sericulture and the weaving of silk were first developed in China perhaps as early as 2000 B.C. Though techniques for silk manufacture were supposed to be a closely guarded secret, details reached Japan in the first wave of arts transmitted there. Because Japan's aristocracy preferred Chinese products, however, Japan's silk industry did not gain prominence until the Tokugawa era, when the shoguns discouraged foreign trade.

As silk remained the fashionable thread for the aristocracy's fine garments, the Japanese hurriedly turned attention to improving their native industry. By 1740, Japanese silks were of such high quality that they were known even in Europe. When trade finally was inaugurated with the West, Japanese silks were among the most desired commodities.

Sericulture begins with the raising of silkworms and involves more than a dozen carefully controlled stages designed to produce the strongest, most uniform threads. For every six pounds of reeled thread suitable for weaving, silkworms must consume the leaves of some thirty mature mulberry trees. Until the end of the last century, every phase of production was done by hand in thousands of rural homesteads.

The goddess Amaterasu (left), is sometimes credited with giving Japan the gift of the silkworm. More likely, the silkworm was introduced at the end of the third century by Korean and Chinese immigrants. Immediately below, a scene depicting silkworm cultivation. Workers variously chop and pack mulberry leaves as well as feed them to the worms, which are kept in bamboo baskets during this stage of production.

Following a forty-two-day feeding period, the worms set about wrapping themselves in the continuous silk fibers that make up the cocoons (below). Cocoon spinning takes eight days, after which drying must begin.

Right, silk workers steam a number of cocoons over fire to suffocate the chrysalis, or worm, within each one. Once the chrysalis is dead, the cocoon is air-dried for several weeks after which the thread that forms can be wound onto a reel.

Above, silk workers preparing skeins before dyeing. A guidance device prevents the threads of different reels from tangling, enabling the worker to prepare ten skeins by turning a single handle. In an earlier step, reels were prepared by winding the filaments of six or seven cocoons together to form a single, stronger thread.

Having dyed the skeins, the weaver produces the finished fabric (right). By working the seven-foot treadles to raise and lower the lengthwise threads in varying combinations, the weaver was able to create remarkably intricate patterns.

tions," and that culminated over fifty years later in a full code of laws known as the Taihō codes. He declared that all agricultural land would cease to be the property of wealthy individuals and clans and would become the property of the state. Some of the land would be allocated to the nobility as "office" or "rank" land, a form of remuneration for services performed, but the majority was to be divided into small parcels and distributed to the general populace, the amount in each case to be determined by the size of a man's family with credits being given for each male over six years of age. Members of be communities were to be freed from obligation to an uji and would

pay taxes—in the form of rice, handicrafts, and labor, including military service—to the state on a systematic basis set according to the assessed value of the land held. Periodic censuses would readjust land distribution to reflect local changes in population.

To administer this vast territory efficiently, land and citizens were to be further organized into provincial, county, village, and neighborhood units, the latter being communes of five peasant families, each of which was responsible for carrying out the directives of the imperial administrators above it.

Though the aristocracy was nominally stripped of its chief source of wealth—land and the services pre-

The many temples in Kyōto, Japan's imperial capital from 794 to 1868, symbolize the beauty of Japan. Left, the pagoda of Kiyomizu-dera, built in 1633 on the site of the original eighth-century compound. Below left, an interior view of a hall in the Nishi Hongan-ji, built in 1272. Below, a guardian of the Daigo-ji, first built in 874 on a rocky peak on Mount Hiei, northeast of Kyōto, but later dismantled and rebuilt at the foot of the mountain.

Right, a tranquil passage through a garden pond in Kyōto. Ponds, together with artificial islands or stones carefully placed in the water, are essential features of most classical gardens, symbolizing the position of the country itself within the earthly oceans. Here a steppingstone path is characteristically made crooked to slow the user's step, forcing him to reflect on the beauties around him. Following pages, the Ginkaku-ji, or Silver Pavilion, built by the eighth shogun, Ashikaga Yoshimasa, in 1474 near Kyōto. Like the superb Kinkaku-ji, or Golden Pavilion, erected in 1397, Yoshimasa's villa is chiefly a viewing tower from which to contemplate surrounding gardens.

Below, Mounted Warrior, *Tosa school of painting. The Tosa were a hereditary line of scroll painters, dating from medieval times and flourishing under the Ashikaga shoguns. Their principal subjects were secular events and historical personages.*

The making of swords, which reached a high state of technical excellence in the feudal era, as this long sword (right) demonstrates, was as highly respected as painting. A samurai's two swords were not only his principal weapons; they were also regarded as having a kami, *or soul, and when he retired from the field, he frequently had them enshrined in a temple with other sacred relics. Based on the shape of the tip, this sword is classified as an* O-kissaki, *or Long Point.*

viously rendered by the be in the territory of the aristocracy—the reforms were in fact designed to balance the loss by giving the most powerful men stipends, lucrative new posts, and compensatory titles in government. That the old eminent families resisted these sweeping changes so little suggests that they were less affected than the terms of the reforms would have seemed to indicate. They now had the centralized authority of the emperor to assure them of their privileged rank, albeit a rank with new titles, and they could look to the emperor to see that taxes were collected and order kept. Regrettably for Japan's future, there was still too little effort expended to place men

of special merit or abilities in positions of importance. Heredity remained the principal measure of a man's worth. With regard to the outlying areas of Japan, little or no effort was made to impose change; uji chiefs scarcely recognized the imperial government and continued to run their states as they had for centuries.

One important trapping of government Japan lacked was a capital, a fixed residence for the sovereign, such as the Chinese had established long ago. Traditionally, in entirely rural Japan, the functions of government centered around the personal estate of

whoever was emperor at the time. As all candidates were drawn from the Sun Line, who had lived for generations in or around Yamato, the "capital" was always a village somewhere within that region. Imperial palaces tended to be scarcely more imposing than the small thatched huts that clustered around them, and whenever a sovereign died his palace was regarded as impure and was abandoned.

After much consultation with Shinto and Buddhist priests as well as Chinese geomancers, the old injunction was rejected, and in 710 a site for Japan's first city and permanent capital was chosen on the northern end of the Yamato plain, at a village named Nara, where two great Buddhist temples already stood. Nara grew quickly and for the next seventy-five years flourished as the focal point of Japanese court life, of secular and religious learning, and of the creative arts. The city itself was a self-conscious copy on a reduced scale of Changan, the capital of Tang China, with broad avenues laid out upon a rigid grid plan and handsome state buildings made of wood according to the Chinese taste.

The first stirrings of a native literature produced the *Kojiki*, "Records of Ancient Matters" (in 712), and the *Nihon Shoki*, the official chronicles of Japan (in 720), as well as the first great collection of poetry,

The cult of the samurai

At the center of the feudal system were the samurai, or gentlemen warriors. They originally constituted a class of arms-bearing independent landowners who fought for their local government official or military leader in time of war in return for protection and later a grant of land. In time, however, they gave up their property rights in exchange for a modest salary and membership in a highly honored professional caste. They were bound in a rigid chair of command to their immediate superior, usually a *daimyo*, or lord, and they took their rules of conduct from an unwritten code known as *bushido*, the Way of the Warrior. Loyalty to their lord and readiness for combat were paramount virtues to the samurai.

The samurai faced a life of considerable hardship and frugality in which his principal possessions might be no more than his elaborate suit of armor and his swords. His residence for years at a time would be away from family at the castle of his daimyo. He proudly apprenticed at a young age with a master of archery and swordsmanship, and he equipped himself with the finest weapons he could find. Each samurai was permitted by law to own two swords—a long steel blade with a two-handled hilt for swashbuckling contact on horseback or foot and a short sword for finishing off the enemy in close encounters or perhaps for committing *seppuku*, ritual self-disembowlment, if he dishonored himself by failing to measure up to the warriors' code.

This full suit of lacquered leather armor (near right) was designed for a sixteenth-century samurai. It includes a half mask, shoulder guards, thigh armor, and leggings, indicating that its owner fought on foot. The breastplate was his personal identification. Above far right, a suit of similar vintage. The elaborate knot at back kept the shoulder guards from falling forward. The bowl helmet has an opening for the warrior's top knot of hair. Below far right, an iron and wood helmet. Long in back, it gave the wearer some added protection against decapitation.

Though the samurai normally wore several layers of clothing, including hakama *(billowing pantaloons), shinguards, helmets, and chainmail sleeves when going into battle, this painting (above) illustrates how the urban military elite dressed in Edo Japan during times of peace. The samurai has his two swords at the ready and assumes a formidable pose. Right, various stirrups for mounted warriors, affording them instant release when they needed to dismount. The figures below are statuettes depicting the warriors in the traditional salutation observed before Kendō meetings, gatherings of men training in the martial arts.*

Zen

Of the many Buddhist sects that took root in Japan, Zen, first preached in the twelfth century, was one of the most influential, having as its principal followers a large segment of the military caste. Zen emphasized discipline, frugality, meditation, and reliance on self in the pursuit of *satori,* or spiritual enlightenment. In contrast to the teachings of other sects, Zen taught that satori might come in a sudden flash to one who was capable of clearing his mind of ordinary logical thought processes. *Kōans,* deliberately enigmatic problems, were presented by Zen masters to their students in the belief that focusing on such problems could lead to transcendental insights. Kōans were meditated upon for many hours at a time in the *zazen,* or cross-legged position. For men whose secular lives were devoted to warfare and who lived with the constant specter of death, such contemplative and tranquil pursuits were highly valued.

Above, Ikkyū Sōjun (1394–1481), a famous Zen priest as well as writer and painter, shown in a contemporary portrait by Bokusai. During his lifetime, he and other Zen masters were closely associated with the Ashikaga shoguns, who transformed their sect into an all but official organ of government. Zen priests and monks functioned as political counselors to the bakufu, as diplomats, and as legal and financial experts. They ran Japan's chief center of classical Chinese studies, thereby controlling much of the intellectual life of the aristocracy.

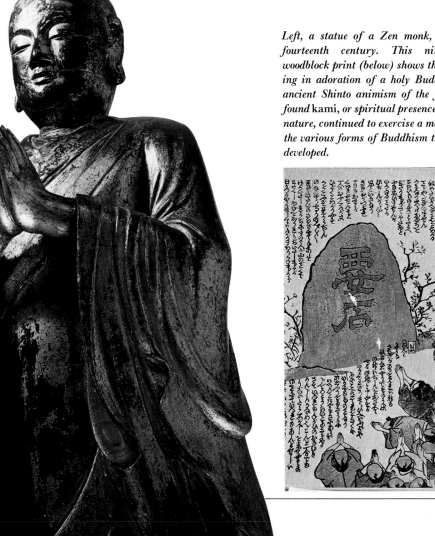

Left, a statue of a Zen monk, sculpted in the fourteenth century. This nineteenth-century woodblock print (below) shows the faithful kneeling in adoration of a holy Buddhist stone. The ancient Shinto animism of the Japanese, which found kami, *or spiritual presence, in every part of nature, continued to exercise a major influence on the various forms of Buddhism that subsequently developed.*

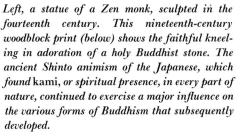

The courtyard of the Ryoan-ji Temple, Kyōto (above), is generally considered the sublime example of the Zen art of garden design. Its counterpoint of five rock and moss islands within a sea of coarse white sand is intended to encourage meditation as a believer gazes out upon its pure expanse. This priest has just completed the daily ritual of raking the sand into patterns symbolizing the waves of the sea; he leaps deftly over the area completed to avoid disturbing a single grain.

Right, a garden of the Daisen-in, one of several "dry stone" gardens within the Daitoku-ji complex in Kyōto. This small configuration of rocks and plants is meant to represent rugged mountain peaks and a wild countryside. Certain rocks of particular beauty have over the centuries held such favor that it was not uncommon for a powerful member of the aristocracy to donate a particular specimen to a temple as an act of piety. This particular garden dates from about the sixteenth century, when the temple complex was built.

Left, Zemmui, a patriarch of the Tendai sect of Buddhism, in an eleventh-century ink on silk painting. Bishamon, god of war, attends. This kakebotoke, *or votive disk (above), dating from the Kamakura era, depicts the Buddha.*

the *Manyōshu* (ca. 759), containing over forty-five hundred poems, usually written in Chinese characters to represent native Japanese sounds, and evidencing a distinctly Japanese view of the world. Sculpture, painting, music, and thought were all devoted to the veneration of the great Buddha.

On the surface the Nara period was a golden age for Japan, but behind the scenes, at the peasant level, the land reforms lately instituted were already going awry. At the foundation of Nara's prosperity was a system of taxation so burdensome to peasants that it drove many farmers off their land and into serfdom, forcing them to turn over their holdings to the few remaining large landholders. As the peasant land allocations were taken over by wealthy landowners who were partially exempt from paying taxes, the land rendered less and less income to the state. State land holdings were further reduced by the practice of granting favors in the form of land gifts to members of the aristocracy when for some reason they pleased the emperor. Temples also gained additional partially tax-exempt lands from the members of the imperial family whenever one of them was moved to donate land to gain favor with the gods. With fewer and fewer acres to tax each passing year, individual levies against the few land-owning peasants became

still more intolerable and caused tensions to mount.

The escalation of taxation on the peasants had an erosive effect on the central government. As imperial power diminished, monasteries became more assertive; some began to behave like independent principalities, with laws and even armies of their own. It was not unknown for priests to involve themselves in palace intrigues with ambitions of gaining the throne, particularly during a succession of female rulers in the eighth century.

The Fujiwara tolerated the erosion of imperial authority until 781, when they rallied behind Emperor Kammu in a plan to move the capital to a new site, beyond the influence of Nara's priesthood. Three years after Kammu's accession, construction was begun on a new palace at Nagaoka, a village northeast of Nara. In the remarkably brief period of five months and with crippling expenditures of money and men that they could ill afford (it was said that three hundred thousand laborers worked day and night), the Imperial Palace was completed and work was begun on building roads and bridges.

Before the actual transfer from old to new capital was completed, however, Kammu and his advisors had second thoughts about the auspiciousness of their choice and issued an edict specifying yet another site for the future royal residence: Heian-kyo, later called

The Kamakura Daibutsu, or Great Buddha (above), was cast in 1252 and portrays in meditative form Amida Buddha, who reigns in the Western Paradise. Originally housed in a temple, it stands today in the open air. Left, Amida Nyorai, in didactic pose, hands raised. Nyorai refers to the Buddha who has achieved total enlightenment.

Kyōto, or Capital, just five miles north of Nagaoka. Once again thousands of men were thrown into the task of building palaces, temples, and roads. Late in 795 the new "Capital of Peace and Tranquility" was ready to receive the emperor and his retinue. Nara, in the meantime, was summarily abandoned to the priests.

Emperor Kammu had been one of the few emperors to rule as well as reign in Japan and the last to do so for a very long time. Despite the appearance of continued strength, the imperial throne was fast losing power and authority to the prolific Fujiwara clan. It was the Fujiwara, not Kammu's successors, who came to shape Japanese government policy, set taxes, regulate trade, and appoint provincial officials. Generation after generation, the Fujiwara offered their

Above, the monk Nichiren, founder of the nationalistic Nichiren, or Lotus, sect of Buddhism, calming the tempest. He is on his way to exile on the island of Soto, having incurred the authorities' wrath by calling their Buddhism heretical. Nichiren was eventually permitted to return to his people, and he retired to Mount Fuji in 1274.

daughters as wives to the imperial family; they would then persuade their emperor sons-in-law to retire in favor of their heirs, usually at an age when the heirs were too young to rule in their own right and needed a regent, a role the Fujiwara gladly filled. Intermarriage was so total that virtually the only genealogical distinction between the imperial clan and the Fujiwara was the former's unique and essential claim to divinity as descendants of Amaterasu, the sun goddess. Each successive emperor, taken up with ever more complex court protocol rituals and with responsibilities as the nation's chief priest, seems to have willingly abdicated his political role. The Fujiwara, by contrast, were energetic and effective administrators, and the dual system of government that developed worked reasonably well in the more settled parts of the country.

Problems were still prevalent in the area of land ownership. In an ill-conceived effort to reverse the trend of the peasants' relinquishment of their land to a few landowners, the government reinstituted private ownership of some uncultivated lands, offering incentives in the form of several years of tax-free status to anyone willing to clear and irrigate them. These newly cultivated, privately owned lands were called *shoen,* or manors. Since such projects usually required considerable capital outlay, only those already-wealthy landowners could take advantage of the offer, thus further enhancing the land wealth of the rich at the expense of the poor—and ultimately undermining the central government's strength.

The aristocratic families, naturally enough, grew complacent—too satisfied as it turned out. Life in the region around Kyōto was so pleasant that many all but ignored their provincial estates, turning management over to administrators drawn from junior branches of their family who, for one reason or another, were not part of the inner circle. Members of the Kyōto court were thus free to immerse themselves in the brilliant yet decadent social and cultural life of the capital.

Kyōto society was preoccupied with form and ceremony. The good life consisted largely of the pursuit of aesthetic and physical pleasures, against a back-

Above, the Mongol invaders—150,000 strong—on the eve of their second attack on Japan in June 1281, approaching the northern coast of Kyūshū in Korean ships. The Japanese armies gather along the newly completed stone wall (below), their swords sharpened to await the dreaded landing. Fifty days of fierce conflict followed in which neither side could break the other's resistance. Then, a kamikaze, or divine wind, swept the coast in the latter part of August, routing the enemy fleet and assuring a Japanese victory.

ground of pageantry, picnics, poetry reading, and superb gardens. All conduct was governed by considerations of good taste, and the minutest details of life—from behavior in court toward persons of lower rank to conducting a romantic liaison to the picking of one perfect flower—were governed by a peculiarly Japanese sense of decorum and rightness. Noticeable too was the decline in direct Chinese influence; since Nara times, mainland models had been so thoroughly absorbed into the culture as to be no longer consciously imitated.

The vacuum thus created by the aristocracy's withdrawal from its responsibilities was destined to bring widespread social problems. The provincial administrators were often as overworked as they were corrupt and rapacious. They were expected to supervise vast lands and thousands of peasants in raising crops and to provide protection in the form of arms and leadership when, as increasingly happened, clashes arose with their neighbors. They were also obliged to come to the emperor's aid when needed.

After performing for years under these demanding conditions they began to seize opportunities for improving their situation. Their eventual rise to the top of a class of military leaders together with their personal retinues of samurai (land-owning warriors who served as their retainers) marked the beginning stage of what is known as feudal Japan, an era that would last more than seven centuries and set the tone for most of what we consider to be traditional Japanese culture today.

Truly native culture began to emerge as a dramatic force only in Kyōto. By the beginning of the tenth century, Kana (a phonetic script or syllabary) was developed to take the place of the purely Chinese system of ideographs that had proved poorly suited to the writing of the Japanese language. Japanese literature and history could now be set down in a form available to a far wider audience. No longer would the court aristocracy have exclusive access to this powerful tool; educated men in the provinces might also learn to read and write. Architecture and art also gave witness

to original, indigenous impulses in this period, the best-known examples being the popular style of secular scroll painting known as *Yamato-e,* or "Japanese-style painting."

Buddhism, too, found a wider audience, despite the effort of the court to curb the influence of some of its priests. The two main Chinese-inspired sects of Tendai and Shingon had long enjoyed a wide following among the aristocracy, and each was distinguished by rigid adherence to Chinese doctrine and the promise of salvation through meditation and moral perfection. In addition, numerous native sects of even broader appeal sprang up in feudal Japan. Pure Land, True Pure Land, and Nichiren, for example, promised salvation through faith alone. All were able to explain themselves in texts written in the new Kana, and all drew their clergy and their inspiration from humble native roots. Adherence to the newer sects was a mark of many in the military caste, providing yet another distinction and source of conflict between the Heian court and the large landholding,

Oda Nobunaga, one of Japan's great unifiers, was assassinated in 1582 in Kyōto, and had his headquarters in the fortress of Azuchi (left). Toyotomi Hideyoshi (above) led a campaign to avenge Nobunaga's murder, then continued unification, building his own palace headquarters at Momoyama, near Kyōto. Below, a window in a wall of the Great Audience Hall.

Himeji (left), or White Heron, so called for its white plaster walls, is a typical example of castle architecture of the feudal era. Parts of the fortress were built in 1581 by Hideyoshi, and it assumed its finished form in 1609 when Tokugawa Ieyasu gave it to one of his daimyo vassals. Another example, Fukashi castle (right), built on the Matsumoto plain, was begun in 1504 and completed in 1594. Notably dramatic are its wide-reaching snow roofs, which produce strong patterns of light and shade. The arrowheads (below left) were fashioned for the warrior aristocracy in the Tokugawa era.

samurai-warrior caste in the adjacent countryside.

Conflict or not, the Fujiwara found themselves growing increasingly dependent on the skills of the military men they had so long scorned. One warrior clan, the Minamoto, had managed to draw into its circle a host of other warriors with their retinue, until it constituted a league of armies of far greater might than the emperor claimed under his own banner. Rather than clash with this fearsome league of fighters, the Fujiwara entered into an alliance with them. At times the central government also requested the aid of the Taira, another similarly constituted league, in driving back the pirates who were successfully waylaying imperial tax shipments on the Inland Sea.

The two leagues inevitably came face to face in the middle of the twelfth century at the invitation of rival groups in Kyōto. The stage for this bloody conflict had been set in the latter half of the eleventh century when the Fujiwara's usual success in supplying the emperor with a wife failed. A new imperial ruler, Sanjō II, ascended the throne in 1068. He owed no allegiance to the clan that had so long served as the state's chief counselor. Unlike his recent predecessors, Sanjō showed a surprising appetite for rule. Nonetheless, four years of trying to exercise authority from the throne convinced him that there was no escape from the debilitating burden of ceremonial duties and court intrigues, so he abdicated in 1072 in favor of his son. Sanjō became a priest and proceeded to govern in retirement through his young heir Shirakawa, thus initiating a new system of government called *insei,* or "cloistered rule."

Sanjō died the following year before his scheme for running a "cloistered" government could be fairly tested, but Shirakawa was persuaded to try the same ploy. He soon retired to rule indirectly as did a number of his successors over the next hundred years. Now the machinery of real and sham government was even more complex than it had been. Inevitably, "cloistered" emperor, enthroned puppet, and Fu-

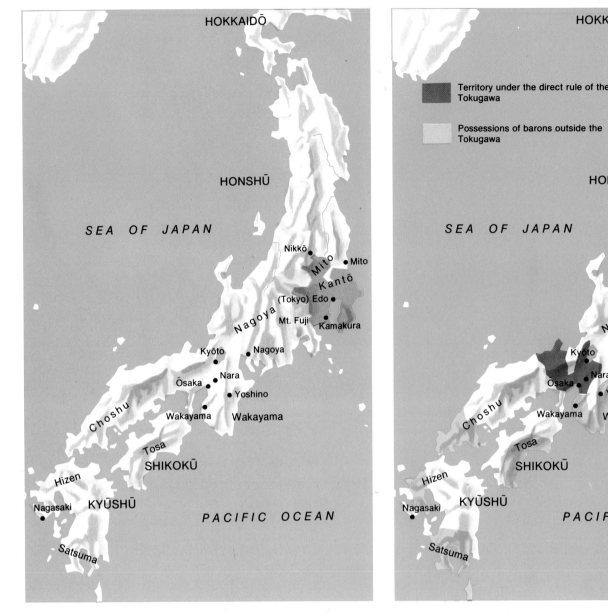

Japan during the twelfth century

A visitor to Japan during the Heian era (794–1192) would have noticed the great influence that China exercised on Japanese society of the time. During the Kamakura era (1185–1333), however, the two societies were drawn far apart. Another important development of this period was the transfer of power from the aristocracy to the samurai, or warrior, class.

In the twelfth century power rested in the hands of two families—the Minamoto in the east and the Taira in the west. They eventually clashed openly in a dispute between the reigning emperor and retired emperors known as the Hōgen War (1156).

The Heiji War (1159–1160) soon followed, once again pitting the Taira against the Minamoto. As before, the Taira triumphed, but the setback for the Minamoto proved only temporary. Sensing the difficulties the Taira were having in exercising control, the Minamoto seized the opportunity to rebuild their power. Led by the brilliant leader Yoritomo, they tested their strength against the ailing Taira in the Gempei War (1180–1185). The Minamoto victory signaled the permanent defeat of the Taira and the start of rule by the samurai class.

Japan during the Tokugawa period [1603-1868]

The Tokugawa period, which began when Ieyasu took power in 1603, was marked by an unbroken peace that endured for 265 years. During this era, Japan experienced significant economic growth and saw the rise of a flourishing urban culture. As a means of safeguarding the peace, Japan's rulers virtually shut the door to all foreigners and imposed a rigid system of social stability at home.

The political system devised by Ieyasu, in which many *daimyo*, or feudal lords, lost all or part of their holdings, enabled the Tokugawa to triple the size of its own holdings by the middle of the seventeenth century. This increase was accompanied by a growth in the size of Tokugawa cities.

To ensure control over the cities and villages of Japan, a rigid class system was established in which the samurai occupied the dominant position, with artisans, peasants, and merchants in subordinate roles. Control was also strengthened by isolating Japan from the outside world. Fearing the impact that Christianity would have on the population, the country's leaders mandated a policy of national seclusion beginning in the 1630s that was to remain in effect for over two hundred years.

Japan after the Russo-Japanese War [1905]

With the arrival of Commodore Matthew C. Perry in 1853, Japan began reopening its doors to the West. In 1854 the Tokugawa family signed a treaty with Perry that permitted American ships to enter the ports of Shimoda and Hakodate. Soon after, Great Britain, Russia, and the Netherlands concluded similar agreements.

The approval of these treaties provoked widespread resentment among Japan's citizens. Riots broke out during which foreigners were killed and their possessions destroyed. Popular discontent coupled with a steady weakening of Tokugawa authority provided government opponents with an opportunity to bring to power a new regime and restore the emperor to his throne.

During the reign of Emperor Mutsuhito (1867–1912), Japan undertook a wide-ranging program of reform. The capital was moved to Edo and renamed Tokyo, a state-controlled system of education was instituted, and feudalism was abolished. Most important, the nation began a period of intense modernization.

Japan's transformation into a modern state was accompanied by imperialistic expansion. Rivalries soon developed between China and Japan that led to the Sino-Japanese War of 1894–1895. The clash of Japanese and Russian interests in Asia led to Japan's declaring war on Russia in 1904. Under the terms of the Treaty of Portsmouth (1905) Russia acknowledged Japan's supremacy in Korea and ceded the Liaotung Peninsula in China. Japan also acquired the southern half of Sakhalin Island.

Relations between Japan and Korea were frequently stormy, beginning ca. A.D. 200, when the semimythical empress Jingo (right) was said to have subjugated her mainland neighbor. The carp in the painting symbolizes her male child, held by the minister (foreground). Son Ōjin was posthumously deified Hachiman, god of war and patron deity of the Minamoto. Left, a painting depicting a Japanese invasion of Korea by Toyotomi Hideyoshi, in 1592. Above, Yi Sun-shin, the Korean who turned the Japanese back at the Yalu River.

jiwara counselors began to gather rival forces behind them.

A struggle over succession to the throne broke out in 1156 when the now desperate Fujiwara called in the Minamoto and their followers to be their "teeth and claws," as they so vividly put it. The Minamoto met the still more powerful Taira league, representing the "cloistered" emperor and another imperial claimant, in a bloody series of wars that erupted within the capital. The chief of the Minamoto and his leading officers either were killed or, facing defeat, committed ritual *harakiri,* the traditional warrior's suicide by disembowelment. Much of the city burned to the ground.

The Taira chieftain Kiyomori stepped forward to replace the Fujiwara counselor as the official minister to the throne, and rule by a "cloistered" emperor resumed. The Taira made the fatal mistake, however,

of modeling their behavior on that of the deposed Fujiwara. They so thoroughly immersed themselves in court life that they soon lost touch with the source of their original strength—the provincial chieftains and samurai—and were in the end abandoned by them.

The remnants of the Minamoto went into hiding in the provinces until they had gathered sufficient strength to seek revenge. Then, beginning in 1180, they struck back under the leadership of Minamoto Yoritomo, and for nearly five years Japan was convulsed with war, destruction, and widespread suffering, as the Minamoto waged war against their Taira enemies. Finally, in 1185, the Taira together with the boy-emperor Antoku met the Minamoto in a decisive battle at Dannoura on the Inland Sea. The Taira fleet sank, its leaders and the youthful emperor drowned, and the ancient system of government toppled.

The Minamoto were now in complete charge. Yoritomo acted boldly and with originality. Leaving the Fujiwara and the emperor to continue as guardians of classical culture and as ceremonial figureheads for a virtually emasculated throne in Kyōto, the commander in chief set up the real government—henceforth known as the *bakufu,* or headquarters—in the isolated fishing village of Kamakura, not far from modern Tokyo. To legitimize his own role, Yoritomo forced the "cloistered" emperor to make him the first of a hereditary line of shoguns, an abbreviation of *seii taishogun* meaning "barbarian-quelling generalissimo." He then staffed his new government with professional military retainers drawn from the ranks of the samurai.

When Yoritomo died in 1199, his wife conspired to bring her father's family, the Hojo, into control of the shogunate. For the next hundred years the military dictatorship functioned with a Minamoto shogun as figurehead for a Hojo regent, the real ruler. This two-stage authority was a mirror image of the emperor-regent system established in Kyōto, except that at the end of the chain of command the Hojo, unlike the Fujiwara imperial regent, did indeed have the final word.

The Hojo met with little difficulty until 1274 when Kublai Khan, leader of the fearsome Mongols of central Asia, made preparations to launch an attack on the island empire. The Mongols were thwarted twice by bad weather during the five-year battle, however, and the *kamikaze,* the divine wind, finally destroyed their fleet and gave the Japanese a decisive victory in August of 1281. The Japanese took the victory as a sign that they were a favored people.

But for the Kamakura regime victory had been

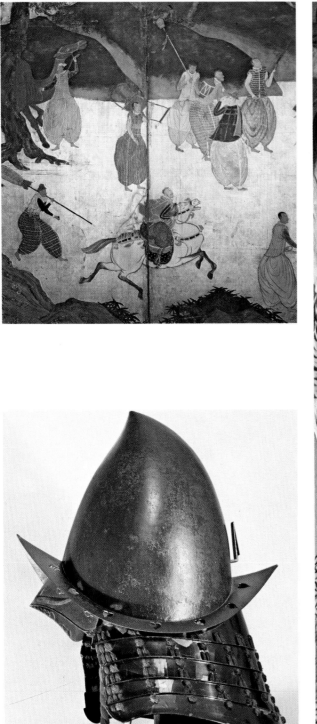

costly. Five years of uninterrupted military service had left the samurai impoverished and discontent, and victory yielded no lavish spoils to replenish revenues lost on untended estates. Their loyalty to the Kamakura government was sufficiently weakened to make them ripe for defection. Many had resumed their traditional lord-vassal relationship with a provincial military governor or with one of the renascent landlord families. Sometimes these individuals found their own interests in conflict with those of the Kamakura generals.

The decisive test of samurai loyalty to the Kamakura government came upon the accession to the

throne of Daigo II in 1318, in Kyōto. Daigo was determined to restore imperial authority to prefeudal levels. To do so, he had to challenge the bakufu, the shogun, and his Hojo regent. When Daigo's intentions were discovered, the bakufu had him imprisoned and exiled to a small island far off the north coast of Honshū, where it was presumed he could cause no further trouble. But a group of lords and Buddhist leaders, supported by samurai, declared themselves loyal to the emperor. Having raised an army, they marched upon Kamakura in 1331. When the bakufu sent its own force to meet them, the shogunate's hand-picked general, Ashikaga Takauji,

Above and above far left, the arrival of the Portuguese on the island of Tanegashima, south of Kyūshū, in 1543. The Portuguese were received with a mixture of curiosity and fear, but their bizarre costumes were an inspiration for Japanese painters. Paintings portraying Westerners became a genre known as namban, *after the Japanese name for the Portuguese "barbarians from the south." Namban styles even inspired changes in fashion, as in the* kabuto *(below far left), a time-honored helmet here copied from a Portuguese model.*

switched sides. He stormed the military capital, killing the Hojo, the puppet shogun, and followers.

But if Daigo thought he could now achieve his imperial goals, he was quickly disappointed. The ambitious Takauji drove Daigo from Kyōto and set up another member of the imperial family as his figurehead. The new emperor obligingly named Takauji as founder of a line of hereditary shoguns. Takauji reestablished the bakufu in a district of Kyōto known as Muromachi, from which the second stage of Japan's feudal era derives its name.

Takauji's victory was not total, however. Some military governors continued to recognize the deposed Daigo, who held rival court south of Honshū on the mountainous island of Shikoku. Still other military governors and their vassal samurai scarcely recognized either the northern or southern courts, operating as lords of some sixty nearly autonomous outlying feudal states. With control at an all-time low, with many ambitious and armed men contending for land, labor, loyalty, and power, local civil wars became a chronic condition.

The weakness of Japan's political institutions during this second phase seems, ironically, to have stimulated dramatic rearrangements of social structure and with it rapid growth in other spheres. Although the Ashikaga shoguns were generally failures as statesmen, they were often exceptional patrons of the arts. Like some of the Heian emperors, they attracted distinguished painters, poets, musicians, architects, priests, and intellectuals to Kyōto. On a smaller scale, but equally important to the development of Japanese culture as a whole, wealthy military governors in the provinces emulated the shoguns by supporting the arts. And everywhere national and international trade was growing, stimulating the expansion of road construction, cities, banking, and coinage as well as classes of merchants and artisans.

During the Ashikaga shogunate, which lasted from 1338 to 1568, the cult of the tea ceremony was formalized, the new Zen-inspired monochrome style of ink-splash painting was developed, architecture reached a peak of naturalism, contemplative gardens of rarified and mystical beauty flourished, and the Nō drama—a highly stylized theater of suggestion combining dance, music, and verse—came into being.

Riches of the spirit could not, however, forestall a major conflict indefinitely. In 1467 the pattern of small localized wars turned into a large civil engagement called the Ōnin War. Nominally, the issue was once again succession, this time to the shogunate of Ashikaga Yoshimasa. Perhaps the greatest of the Muromachi art patrons, Ashikaga was also the worst of a poor lot of statesmen. The war waged intermittently in and around Kyōto for ten years, then shifted to the provinces where it continued for another two decades. By the end of the century, warfare had brought the bakufu and the imperial rulers to the edge of bankruptcy.

Long-established military governors were scarcely more secure. Their samurai, worn by incessant turmoil, repeatedly challenged their vassalage. Some of the dissidents even allied themselves with radical elements within the rural peasant communities, thus encouraging a democratic rebellion that became so widespread as to inspire a new word, *gekokujo*, meaning "inferiors overcoming superiors." A new class of independent civil war barons, *sengoku daimyo*, arose, and the old military governors, whose ties had been to the bakufu and the shogunate, virtually disappeared.

The country was closer to total disunity than it had ever been before. It was only a matter of time before one of the new lords would successfully challenge the shaky Ashikaga shogunate, divest it of what little power remained, and attempt to reunify Japan under a single leader. History would show that three great men were needed to complete the task.

Oda Nobunaga was the first to step forward. He was a civil war daimyo with outstanding military gifts and a domain consisting of a large part of Owari Province, near modern Nagoya in southcentral Honshū. In 1568 he captured Kyōto and dispatched the remaining Ashikaga clan. Leaving the position of shogun vacant, perhaps as a calculated show of modesty, he took the title of vice shogun. He then turned his attacks against the Buddhists, especially those sects possessing large armies and excessive secular power. In the next ten years, he subdued the Tendai stronghold on Mount Hiei, demolishing some three thousand buildings and killing most of its twenty thousand priests and soldiers. He also destroyed the troublesome Ikkō sect in northwest Honshū in a similar bloody fashion. Before he was assassinated by one of his own vassals in 1582, he had brought central Japan under his control.

Left, details from a pair of six-fold namban screens, showing a Portuguese merchant and a Jesuit priest. Francis Xavier, founder of the Jesuit order and the first to work among the Japanese, is pictured in the namban above calming a tempest. Xavier landed at Kagoshima, near Nagasaki, in 1549 and opened the first Catholic church at Yamaguchi the next year with the permission of local daimyo who expected trade to follow. By 1587, however, authorities were sufficiently wary of the potentially subversive effect of the missionaries to prohibit Christianity. Persecutions followed, one of the most brutal being the martyrdom at Nagasaki (right).

Command of Nobunaga's armies then passed to Toyotomi Hideyoshi, the brilliant, ambitious son of a peasant, who had in his first forty-six years risen from Nobunaga's sandal-bearer to his top general. From his headquarters at Ōsaka, Hideyoshi continued Nobunaga's drive toward unification. Within three years he had achieved authority over the central daimyo and forged peace alliances with daimyo throughout the rest of Japan. For the first time in two hundred years, Japan had something approaching a national government under a single leader.

Hideyoshi used his authority to institute rigid controls, particularly over the armed peasants and small landholders who had taken advantage of Japan's weakened state to shake off their feudal masters. He instituted a "sword hunt" aimed at disarming the populace, promising to reforge the weapons into a gigantic Buddha that would see to their protection. He ordered a new land survey designed to reassess the productivity of all farm lands and to establish a new tax base. And to ensure stability within the populace, he promulgated a series of laws fixing social status and domicile, binding, for example, the children of peasants to the land and the children of warriors to the military class.

Hideyoshi had one other pressing problem to solve: what to do with the thousands of newly unemployed warriors under his command. Perhaps as a temporary solution, he laid grandiose plans for overseas expansion, announcing to the emperor that his generals would take Korea and China. In 1592, while Hideyoshi remained at home, enjoying the adulation of the people and the attentions of a reported three hundred concubines, two hundred thousand of his men crossed the Tsushima Strait and quickly subdued the southern Korean peninsula. But as they marched north toward the Yalu River, they were slowed by heavy guerrilla resistance, giving the Chinese the time they needed to organize a counteroffensive. The Japanese turned back only to engage in a second abortive campaign in 1597. When Hideyoshi died the following year, his armies returned to Japan.

Japanese miniatures

The curious little devices shown on these pages—examples of the *inrō* (case) and its companion the *netsuke* (toggle)—might never have come into favor if the Japanese had thought to put pockets in their kimonos. Had they done so, the tobacco and snuff that the Portuguese introduced in the sixteenth century could have been stowed in the folds of a gentleman's robes. Instead, the inrō and the netsuke became items of high fashion, worn with panache over the sash that held the kimono together. Function dictated size: The netsuke was typically one to three inches high and almost equal in weight to the inrō it counterbalanced. The choices of shape, material, and subject matter were virtually limitless. In time, not only tobacco but also coins, medicines, flint, writing brushes, and ink were carried in these diminutive works of art. When the Japanese shed their kimonos for business suits, the miniatures gradually became obsolete, only to gain a new life as collectors' items in the late nineteenth century.

The netsukes shown here reveal a variety of subjects and materials used in that traditional art form. The three animal figures—the frog, horse, and bear—exemplify the most prevalent genre of netsuke and probably represent folkloric characters. The carved human figures, all remarkable for the expressiveness of their faces and the plasticity of their carving, are drawn from mythical and popular themes.

Right, three complete sets of inrō and netsukes as they were typically assembled. The twisted silk cord looped over the sash. The small bead above the inrō slid up when the wearer wished to lift the cover. The netsuke might be made from wood, bone, jade, or even narwhal tusk; the hollow inrō case was often lacquered.

Hideyoshi left an infant son, Hideyori, as his intended political heir, but the claim had no legal or practical basis, and Tokugawa Ieyasu, pre-eminent among Hideyoshi's daimyo allies, quickly established himself as Japan's new strong man by defeating a coalition of rivals at the battle of Sekigahara in 1600.

Ieyasu had no taste for foreign campaigns, but he was determined to create a political system that was strong and stable enough to survive his own death. Taking the title of shogun, Ieyasu established his new bakufu in the village of Edo (modern Tokyo) where in 1590 he had erected his own castle. Leaving his son in charge of everyday affairs, he turned his attention to administrative reforms. Ieyasu's methods, reactionary at best, ruthlessly repressive at worst, cost Japan dearly in terms of creative growth, but they were remarkably effective in completing national unification.

In a vast program of alleged land reform, the first Tokugawa shogun dispossessed some opposing daimyo, including many of Hideyori's supporters. He relegated others, who had only lately come to his support, to the status of *tozama,* or outer daimyo, reducing their holdings or transferring them to areas where they posed a lesser threat. Confiscated territories, particularly those along certain key land and sea routes or surrounding some major market centers, were given to members of his own Tokugawa clan or to allies who had fought on his side at the battle of Sekigahara. These favored men, henceforth designated *fudai,* or hereditary daimyo, enjoyed a reasonable degree of trust by the new Tokugawa shogunate. The outer daimyo, however, were subjected to constant checks on their loyalty by what amounted to a secret service network.

All daimyo were required to pay lengthy ceremonial visits to Ieyasu's capital biannually and, in many cases, to spend alternate years there. They were also

Though the Tokugawa shoguns maintained their headquarters in Edo, they kept an impressive presence in Kyōto at Nijō Castle (above center). Built ca. 1603 adjacent to the Imperial Palace, Nijō was first occupied by Tokugawa Ieyasu's military governor for the region. Its moat and fortress wall were largely symbolic, the aristocracy having neither the armies nor the inclination to pose a serious threat to the Tokugawa ruling elite. Near right, an example of the popular Tokugawa art form of printmaking. Executed in 1720 by Okumura Masanobu, it recalls an encounter between two folk heroes in the Taira-Minamoto wars of the twelfth century.

Right, Tokugawa-period castles. Top, the Ōrin-dō Pavilion at Katsura, an imperial villa outside of Kyōto. Katsura is considered one of the finest examples of Japanese domestic architecture of any era, combining simplicity of line with the most refined use of natural woods. Center, Nijō Castle. The splendid gate (bottom) leads to the east wing of Nijō.

Above, details on a screen of the Edo period, showing Fūjin, the wind god, and Raiden, the god of thunder, in the guise of a demon. Facing page, top and bottom far right, the Imperial Palace in Tokyo. Built on the site of Edo Castle, it was completed in 1640, only to be destroyed during World War Two, then rebuilt. Facing page, near right, a mime dancing to the accompaniment of a drum in a Shinto rite of Ise Jingū, the ancient shrine dedicated to the worship of the goddess Amaterasu.

obligated to establish their wives and children in lavish Edo households where they might be held as hostages should the daimyo show any taint of disloyalty. A curb was placed on castle building by all except the Tokugawa. The daimyo were required to contribute both money and laborers toward other public works projects, the largest share of the costs being borne by the outer daimyo. The bakufu also put a stop to the practice of the daimyo engaging in foreign trade and issuing currency on their own, thus providing the Tokugawa with two principal sources of wealth upon which the lords had previously depended.

By 1614 only two obstacles prevented full security for the Tokugawa: a pocket of resistance at Ōsaka, where remnants of Hideyoshi and Hideyori's supporters remained, and the growing presence of Christian missionaries and traders in a number of small but influential colonies scattered around the coast. In 1615 Ieyasu successfully marched against Ōsaka, putting an end to further threats from that quarter. But dealing with the Europeans was a more persistent problem, one that continued until after Ieyasu's death in 1616.

The Christians had first appeared in 1543, when Portuguese traders bound for China had been shipwrecked off southern Kyūshū. They were followed six years later by the Spanish-born Jesuit Francis Xavier, the first of dozens of Jesuit and Franciscan missionaries who came to spread the Gospel and to win converts.

At first the Japanese welcomed the Westerners, both for the goods they offered (European firearms were highly prized) and for the religious challenge they posed to the still-powerful Buddhists. These newcomers also brought provocative glimpses of Western science and technology—especially precious in a culture whose own intellectual activities had come to a near standstill. By the time the Spanish and Portuguese were joined by Dutch and English visitors toward the end of the sixteenth century, the Westerners were allowed to set up permanent trading stations.

But in time these odd-looking foreigners began to make the Japanese uneasy. Were they the advance battalions of a European armada of conquest? When as many as three hundred thousand Japanese were discovered to have converted to Christianity, Hideyoshi and then Ieyasu sought ways to turn the outsiders back.

In 1614 Ieyasu announced a plan to evict all mis-

The geisha

A unique product of Japanese social traditions, the geisha class arose during the Tokugawa period to serve the new urban bourgeoisie. Descended from a long and respectable line of courtesans who had entertained the aristocracy at court with dancing, song, poetry reading, and an occasional discrete dalliance, the geisha, or female entertainer, gained a broader definition when entertainment quarters, "nightless cities," were established in such commercial cities as Edo and Ōsaka. Here, wealthy merchants were the geisha's principal clients.

In the best establishments, the geisha might be highly educated as well as gifted in the arts, her principal role being that of a companion in conversation. In the more raffish establishments, she might serve, more frankly, as a sexual object. In either case, she fufilled the need for acceptable diversion in a society strongly governed by notions of moral obligation and social duty.

Above, A Courtesan Getting Out of Bed, *painted by Yamamoto Yoshinobu in 1755. Verses that accompanied the work observe, "At dawn the red petticoat in the bedroom is dazzling." In another view of the* ukiyo *(left), or floating world, painted in 1768 by Haranobu, the courtesan Osen is depicted with a client. Paraphenalia on the low table are related to tea serving, which was Osen's formal livelihood. A poem dedicated to her says, "Who knows when my sleeves began to be drenched with my tears, just as the maples turn red in autumn," emphasizing the bittersweet side of the geisha's life.*

Above, an eighteenth-century painting of the amusement quarter called the Yoshiwara, or Flower District, in Edo. Restaurants, theaters, geishas, prostitutes, and strolling performers drew crowds of prosperous townsmen all year round.

Below, A Girl Applying Cosmetics to her Neck (ca. 1796) by Utamaro Kitagawa. One of the most prolific painters of the Yoshiwara, Utamaro specialized in idealized female types. The porcelain complexion and the arched brows were essential features of that ideal.

Three geishas (above) from the tea house Choshiya are depicted in this print by Chokosai Eisho. Public tea houses were generally among the more decorous establishments within the floating world, the tea ritual having great aesthetic and philosophic value. A young girl destined for such an occupation might attend a finishing school where she would learn the subtle arts of serving and conversing from an older, experienced geisha. The sumptuous costumes of these women suggest that they have learned their lessons well. Near right, a late nineteenth-century ivory statuette of a geisha of a later generation.

Nō theater

Among the many art forms that developed in feudal Japan, none surpassed in originality the symbolic theater of Nō. Nō drew its traditions from such earlier secular entertainments as *sarugaku* (mime theater) and *dengaku* (Japanese harvest songs), as well as from Shinto and Buddhist didactic plays. It developed as a highly refined art form under Seami, an actor and playwright of the fourteenth century. Nō consists of epic dramas—usually akin to historical romances—presented on a bare stage by two masked actors and perhaps a few subordinate players. Traditionally divided into five parts, the sequence involves the gods, a warrior, a woman, a mad person, and a festive resolution that generally carries some moral truth. Superb costumes, poetic literary speech, gesture, and dance are essential parts of the performance.

Below left, a painting ca. 1723 of the male actor Sanyo Kantaro playing the role of Princess Yaoya Oschichi in the classic Nō drama Arashi Soga, *the tale of a young woman who loses her life in an attempt to bring home her beloved samurai. Immediately below, an actor in the heavily stylized impasto make-up typically worn in traditional Japanese theater. In the iconography of such performances, the character of the person is revealed by the type of expression he wears. This finely carved mask (bottom), which is lacquered wood in composition, represents one of over a hundred stock Nō character types. Such masks are highly prized today as works of the sculptor's art.*

Against a stark background of tatami *(woven straw mats) and stylized props, contemporary actors (above) perform a Nō drama according to centuries-old modes. Not seen is a chorus that chants portions of the narrative and musicians who play a somber accompaniment on such instruments as the transverse flute, the* tsuzumi *(a small drum played with the finger tips), and the* okawa *(a slightly larger drum played with the fingers).*

Right, an eighteenth-century print depicting *members of the aristocracy gathering at a Nō performance. Despite the festive atmosphere, the play conveyed a tragic view of life. For comic relief, a supplementary* kyōgen, *or comic performance, was customarily given during intermissions. The* kyōgen *is a vestige of the often satirical* sarugaku *(literally "monkey music," or mime) from which Nō developed.*

sionaries from the country. In the next ten years both English and Spanish trading companies withdrew because of increasing restrictions on trade and threats to their safety. The Portuguese were evicted in 1638 following a bloody five-month revolt of Christianized natives on the Shimabara Peninsula on Kyūshū, for which the foreigners were blamed. About the same time, the Tokugawa shogunate forbade Japanese traders to travel outside the country and closed Japanese ports to nationals living abroad. Japanese converts to Christianity were forced to renounce the alien faith or suffer, as thousands did, martyrdom and death. The Japanese were actually forbidden to build ocean-going vessels in an effort to reduce and suppress foreign contact.

Japan had entered a period of national seclusion. Except for occasional visits by Protestant Dutch and Chinese traders (who were permitted to come no closer than the island of Deshima off Nagasaki), there would be no further contact with the outside world for more than two hundred years to come. Christianity as an organized religion also ceased to exist in Japan.

Now the Tokugawa shoguns hoped to take complete control of Japanese society, and they set about fine-tuning the mechanisms of government to ensure success. For their official philosophy, they chose a Chinese school of thought usually termed Neo-Confucianism. This philosophy held that the universe was governed by a set of moral laws at the heart of which was the loyalty of each man to his betters. Where Buddhism had provided a largely other-worldly basis for the behavior of men, Neo-Confucianism stressed reason, order, and law. By 1651, when the third Tokugawa shogun died, the third phase of Japanese feudalism was fully underway, and an immutable class structure determined exactly where each member of Japanese society should be ranked in the strict hierarchy.

Nominally at the top were the imperial descendants of Amaterasu in Kyōto and the court nobility, their kin. The Tokugawa, having decided that the ceremonial function of the imperial family was of value to the regime, had restored a measure of their wealth and prestige, though none of their real power. The shogun, holding a hereditary office drawn from the Tokugawa, stood next in rank, and through outright ownership of or control over forty percent of Japan's arable lands, was both the wealthiest and the most powerful man in the country. Next came the hereditary feudal lords, including junior members of the Tokugawa clan, who were overlords of the choicest domains and eligible for high office. Beneath

them were the outer daimyo, who were not eligible for top political posts but who also derived a generally sizable income from large landholdings. At the bottom of the hereditary ruling class were the samurai, still filling the role of knightly retainers, who were paid in *koku* (a unit of five bushels of rice) by their daimyo in return for serving as officers or foot soldiers. Much of their one-time bravado was gone: Now even their beloved weapons were most likely issued to them by their master. Altogether these top ranks from emperor to horseless samurai constituted no more than ten percent of the population.

The other three classes of society—the peasants, artisans, and merchants—were expected to perform as tributaries to their individual lords, providing the goods and services needed to keep the feudal society functioning, expecting little in return except perhaps the vague promise of protection. As land was the basis of a lord's wealth and rice the main crop as well as the most common unit of value, the peasant-farmer class was both the most numerous and theoretically the highest ranking of the service classes. Of lesser value to the state were those men considered under Neo-Confucian theory to be secondary producers. Such were the artisans, men who fashioned the material goods of society. By the same reasoning, merchants were relegated to yet a lower rank; their role as commercial agents was seen as bordering on economic parasitism.

On the surface this hierarchical structure functioned fairly well. Every class seemed to have accepted its particular role without strong resistance. But like other rigid systems before it, the Tokugawa system did not allow for economic realities. Over the

Below and on facing page, four symbolic screen paintings from the late eighteenth to early nineteenth centuries depicting episodes in Japanese family life and emphasizing the central role played by Buddhist deities. Far left, an altercation between a son and his mother, with a wife or sister attempting to quell the disturbance. Dominating the picture of this lower-class family is a demon, symbol of impending punishment. In the second scene, the family of a noble samurai appears with the three-headed Gosanze Myo Ō, one of the five guardians of the cardinal points.

The third painting also portrays a family of noble caste, guarded by Daikoku, one of the seven gods of luck. On the table is a reproduction of a shimadai, *a miniature landscape given to a bride and groom as a token of good wishes for a happily married life. The mother's costume is decorated with ideograms of* fu *(happiness) and* ju *(longevity). Immediately below, an intoxicated man of lower station, perhaps a shopkeeper. He rails against his wife while his son sleeps peacefully; a malevolent* oni, *or demon, hovers ominously above.*

decades those at the bottom of the structure—particularly the merchants who grew rich speculating in rice and other commodities—came to have unforeseen power over those at the top, allowing them to expect more of the good things of life than their rank actually permitted.

The chief cause of this dislocation of class was the Tokugawa policy of controlling the daimyo by keeping them on the edge of debt. Forced to live on an extravagant scale, to maintain grand households both in their domains and in Edo, to travel constantly with huge retinues befitting their station, and to maintain well-equipped samurai, many borrowed large sums from the merchants. As the daimyo's equity in land was thus ransomed, their unemployed samurai drifted away, often into outlawry, joining roving bands of *ronin*, or masterless warriors. At the same time, the daimyo demanded higher taxes, greater crop allotments, and more labor from the peasants who, pushed beyond endurance, might attempt to disappear into unsettled frontier country or, as happened more and more often, join other resistant peasants in local revolts. And as if these strains were not enough to cause unsettling currents throughout society, the handful of intellectuals among the ruling class who had always resented the Tokugawa policy of seclusion began to intensify their protest.

Meanwhile, Japan's rural economy and dispersed population were slowly being transformed into a more urbanized society. By 1700, perhaps as much as a tenth of the population—mostly of the merchant and artisan classes—were living in cities of over ten thousand people. Scarcely a century after the first Tokugawa had made his castle village at Edo into Japan's political capital, Edo's population had soared to over a half million; by 1750 it had doubled again. Both Kyōto and Ōsaka had, by that time, populations of half a million, and a score of other former castle and temple centers had from fifty thousand to one hundred thousand inhabitants.

Within those cities, merchant guilds fixed credit

rates and controlled the distribution of the majority of products traded in the country. Though the shogunate continued to demand that the ever more prosperous bourgeoisie maintain their stipulated class decorum—plain clothing, quiet pleasures—the townsfolk observed the rules only in token fashion. The wealthy wore rich brocades under their dour outer garments; within their houses they entertained as they pleased. And they patronized amusement quarters called *ukiyos* (floating worlds) that developed in each of the larger cities.

The ukiyo became the center for a new popular culture, distinctly different from the traditional Chinese-inspired culture still preserved by the ruling class. The native kabuki theater—in which resplendently dressed performers acted out melodramas about such themes as domestic conflicts of honor, suicide, and social oppression—became immensely popular, as did *bunraku,* or puppet shows. In geisha houses professional female entertainers offered townsmen another no less popular form of entertainment.

For two hundred years, Nagasaki harbor (left) was the sole Japanese port to receive Westerners, and even then, only one or two Dutch trading ships were permitted each year. Exchanges were initially limited to the fan-shaped island of Deshima (foreground). Except for a few official interpreters, the Japanese were not permitted to learn a foreign language or to receive foreign books. The bakufu gradually eased restrictions, however, permitting Dutch studies and a few Dutch texts to reach a small but receptive audience.

Once the Closed Door was open, Westerners and Japanese discovered they had much to learn from one another. Top, a foreign sailor being initiated into the pleasure of sake, *the national alcoholic drink made from distilled rice. Above, a Dutch steam frigate, the* Soembing, *lying at anchor in Nagasaki harbor while its launch takes men ashore to instruct the Japanese in Western navigation and shipbuilding skills. Both illustrations are examples of* nishiki-e, *or woodblock prints, which were created in great numbers for popular distribution.*

Japan and the West

"The honor of the nation calls for it, and the interest of commerce demands it," wrote Commodore Matthew Perry of the opening of Japan to the West. Perry had been sent as the official representative of the United States government to request from the shogun trading rights for American merchants, and he was fully prepared to use force if necessary to achieve his goals. His tactics, however, were carefully designed to avoid confrontation. Perry made his first stop in the Ryukyus, an archipelago southwest of the Japanese home islands, to set up supply bases for his fleet and to learn more about the people with whom he would soon be dealing. Then, in July 1853, he entered Uraga harbor, delivered a letter from the American president to the emperor, and promised to return the following year for an answer.

In an unprecedented move, a council of ranking daimyo was asked for its opinion by the shogun, as was the emperor. Instructed to refuse Perry, the shogun lamely adopted a policy of compromise. The resultant Treaty of Kanagawa, though modest in its concessions, led the way to ending Japan's long isolation. As other nations pressed for similar privileges—and won them—the majority of daimyo organized a movement to unseat the discredited shogun. Meanwhile, the rising bourgeoisie, and the minority of liberal aristocrats who saw advantages in widening Japan's horizons, welcomed the peaceful invasion with enthusiasm.

The formal ceremonies concluding negotiations for the first treaty of friendship between the Japanese and Americans ended with this banquet (above) on March 31, 1854. In addition to assurances of safe refuge for shipwrecked Americans, the Treaty of Kanagawa won Perry access to the trade ports of Shimoda and Hakodate and the right to set up a permanent American consulate eighteen months hence.

With three steamships, two sloops, and assorted other vessels anchored off Kanagawa, Perry made his second visit to Japan (left), on March 8, 1854. Recognizing the diplomatic value of putting on an impressive show, the commodore mustered more than five hundred sailors and marines in full dress uniform for the event, which was accompanied by a seventeen-gun salute and three marching bands.

Perry's entourage (above) on its preliminary visit to Uraga consisted of four ships. Two of them were painted black and ominously dubbed "The Black Ships" by the Japanese. Perry had read accounts of Japanese customs by earlier European travelers, and he was convinced that his best chance of success lay in keeping a certain awesome mystery about his person. Consequently, no curious Japanese were permitted on board ship, and he refused to communicate with anyone but the accredited emissary of the shogun or emperor.

Relations with traders were periodically disrupted when terrorist attacks by conservative Japanese were met with counterattacks from the opposition. Below, American, French, British, and Dutch warships answer one such incident in September 1864 in the Straits of Shimonoseki. The coastal defenses of the Choshu daimyo were subsequently destroyed by superior Western munitions. In time, the Westerners determined that the shogun was no longer able to prevent recurrences of such attacks, and they took their case to the emperor.

Above, Commodore Matthew Calbraith Perry (1794–1858), in a daguerreotype taken shortly before his departure from home. Americans of that time scarcely acknowledged the event or his achievement. As humorist Finley Peter Dunne (his pen name was Mr. Dooley) put it, "Whin we rapped on the dure, we didn't go in, they come out." Perry and the shogun knew better.

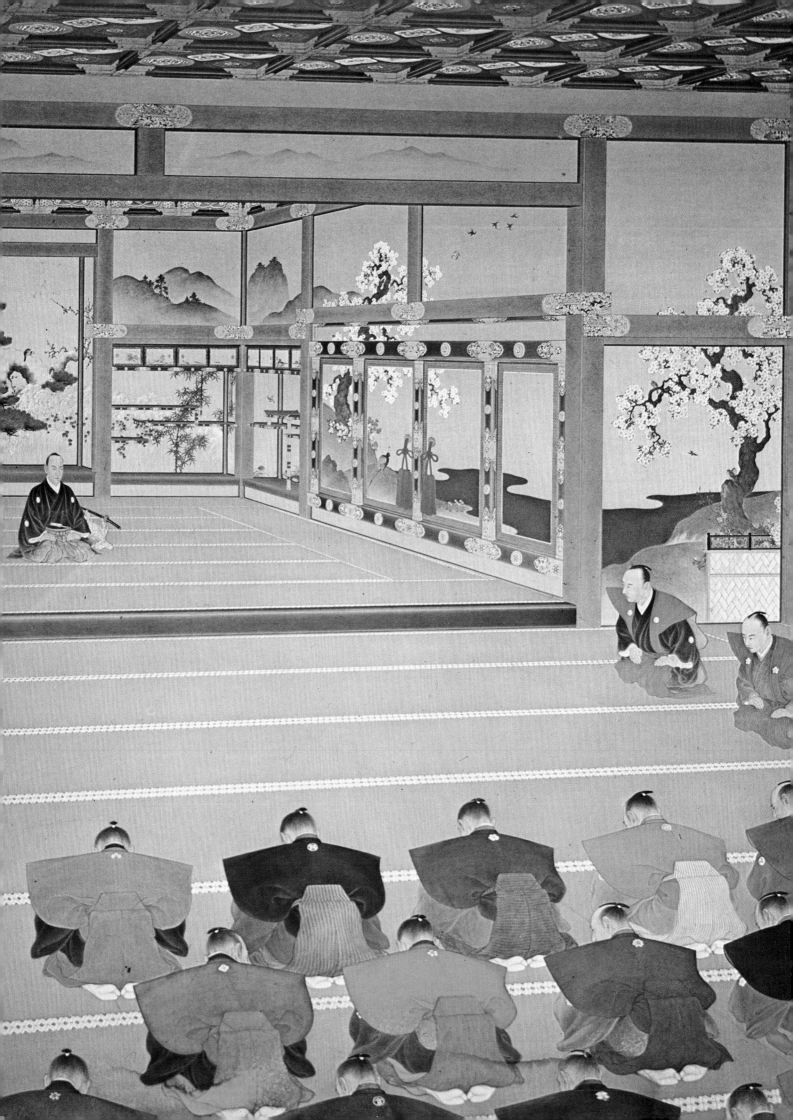

In the graphic arts, woodblock prints, frequently depicting life in the ukiyo, also gained in popularity.

In literature, *haiku*, a poetic form consisting of three lines of seventeen syllables total, became a favored amusement for those seeking a creative challenge, and novel-reading on a popular scale arose as the result of the spread of literacy and the development of printing. Indeed, education—in the form of classroom lectures on Confucian scholarship, as well as studies in Japanese history, Western science, and even anti-feudal philosophy—became available both to samurai and to wealthy merchants. This would contribute significantly to the nation's readiness to modernize in the nineteenth century.

The winds of change were gradually gathering strength all over Asia as Western nations, seeking expanding markets for their goods and new sources of raw materials for home consumption, pressed for contacts. In 1791 two American trading ships made calls, in vain, on Japanese ports. From 1792 onward, the Russians were in the Kuriles, a chain of thirty-two islands stretching from the northeast coast of Hokkaidō to the Far Asian mainland, and subsequent expeditions reached Nagasaki with bids for trade. A British man-of-war entered that city in 1808 and was rebuffed, as was a French fleet in 1846.

Though none of the visitors threatened to open the Closed Door by force, the Tokugawa were sufficiently alarmed to issue a decree entitled *Ni-nen-naku*, or "No Second Thought." It required local officials who were confronted with further brazen visits by Westerners to fire on sight. After the *Morrison*, a friendly American ship bearing Japanese sailors it had rescued en route, was fired on and forced to withdraw without delivering its passengers, the Edo government withdrew the summary rule under heavy criticism at home. It continued, however, to instruct officials to prevent foreigners from landing by whatever means necessary. Knowledge that modern warships of the

Above, the emperor Meiji issuing the "Charter of the Five Articles of the Imperial Covenant" on April 6, 1868, moving Japan into the modern age. Below, Meiji in Western military uniform holding a saber.

Keiki, who became the fifteenth and last Tokugawa shogun in 1867, receives officials in an ornate chamber of the Kuroshoin (left), a hall within the grounds of Nijō Castle, Kyōto. Keiki tried briefly to save the bakufu through concessions to the daimyo, but soon was persuaded that only imperial restoration would prevent civil war. He resigned in November 1867, expecting to become the prime minister, but the following January the shogunate was abolished and Tokugawa lands confiscated, forcing Keiki to bow out.

British Navy had lately defeated the Chinese in the Opium War may have also convinced the Tokugawa to take a somewhat less provocative stance.

In 1853 a powerful American squadron commanded by Commodore Matthew Perry steamed up Edo Bay with a letter from President Millard Fillmore demanding "friendship, commerce, a supply of coal . . . and provisions and protection for our shipwrecked people." The Tokugawa regime was now faced with a diplomatic and political crisis. Realists among them observed that they had no practical way to resist. Yet they knew that to open the Closed Door even a crack was to end forever Japan's seclusion.

Perry informed his reluctant greeting party that he would return for an answer in the spring, bringing a still larger fleet with him. At the appointed time and without securing the emperor's blessing, the Tokugawa leaders ruefully signed a treaty opening two ports—Shimoda on the island of Honshū and Hakodate on Hokkaidō. The document permitted limited trade in those ports and cleared the way for the establishment of an American consulate. Within another two years Great Britain, Russia, and Holland had won similar concessions.

Some Japanese received the news with excitement. Perry's gift to the emperor of a telegraph station and a tiny steam railroad, for instance, had totally astonished the treaty signers. The Kyōto court and many Tokugawa clansmen, however, were so incontrovertibly opposed to the Edo government's concessions that they had the prime minister—whom they held responsible for Japan's losses—assassinated in 1860. Terrorist attacks on foreigners also occurred, prompting a number of retaliatory attacks by Westerners on Japanese ports. Now the court had an issue on which it hoped to regain some power of its own, and it repeatedly demanded that the shogun renounce the treaties and expel the foreigners. Two and a half centuries of Tokugawa repression had created many allies for the emperor and precious few for the current regime. Civil war threatened, only to be resolved peaceably by one of those remarkable concurrences

Facing page, two views of Tokyo in the first decade after westernization. Traditional land vehicles such as jinriksha *have been joined by bicycles on the main bridge leading into the city in this detail (far left) from a woodblock print, ca. 1873. The new citizen army (left), having taken Western uniforms in 1867, parades to the music of Western band instruments on an island in Tokyo Bay, in this woodblock print by Andō Hiroshige, ca. 1870. The army was initially trained and led by Saigō Takomori; later, when he left government to lead the Satsuma Rebellion, it was this army that defeated his ex-samurai dissidents.*

In 1872, service was inaugurated on the Tokyo to Yokohama railroad (above). It boasted eighteen miles of track and ran several times a day. The first Western bank, the Mitsui (left), was launched the same year. The Mitsui family, bankers since 1691, was a major zaibatsu, *or financial clique, that formed after the Meiji Restoration.*

that shape great historic dramas.

In September of 1866, the old shogun conveniently died. Six months later the reigning emperor also passed on. A new young Tokugawa shogun, Keiki, and a new young emperor, Mutsuhito, took their respective places. But before the nation could take the measure of either man, the outer daimyo, led by dissidents in distant Satsuma and Choshu, met to draw up an ultimatum. They demanded that the new Tokugawa chief resign his powers. Keiki was fortunately inclined to their thinking. Aware that the bakufu had lost virtually all popular support, he willingly yielded his title. On January 3, 1868, power was officially restored to the emperor. Shortly thereafter, the rest of the Tokugawa clan, who were awarded princely rank for their cooperation, surrendered their vast land holdings.

The new emperor, only fifteen years old, took as his reigning name *Meiji,* or Enlightened Rule—an appropriate designation for his forty-five year career as emperor. With the guidance of advisors drawn from the ranks of outer daimyo and progressive samurai, Meiji issued a Charter Oath at the outset. Even the shogunate's enemies by now had come to realize that westernization was the only way to preserve Japan's independence in the face of the West's rapid expansion into Asia, and this became the thrust of Meiji's declaration. The imperial oath proclaimed the unity of the state and the people, calling on both to consecrate themselves to the common welfare. It ordered the cessation of "evil customs," a reference to practices that persisted from the feudal era. It removed all restrictions concerning an individual's choice of livelihood, concluding that everyone should have an op-

portunity to realize his talents. Decisions on public matters were to be made in concert with public assemblies, presumably made up of the daimyo and samurai. And knowledge was to be welcomed from all parts of the world to help bring Japan into a position of equity with other nations.

As a symbol of the modern state in the making, the capital was officially moved to Edo and renamed Tokyo. The feudal structure was also dismantled. Daimyo sympathetic to the new regime were the first to be persuaded to return their lands to the state; other daimyo followed suit. In 1871 some three hundred former fiefdoms were recast as seventy-two prefectures and three metropolitan districts, all theoretically under a single, central rule. As for Japan's ancient social structure, virtually every element was redefined. The daimyo, in surrendering their feudal lands, had abolished themselves as a class, though

they received as recompense pensions in the form of interest-bearing government bonds and peerage ranks. Many also won government posts. The samurai, numbering with their dependants nearly two million, gradually lost what traditional rights and privileges they had managed to reserve under the Tokugawa regime. With the introduction of military conscription in 1872, they lost their unique position as the nation's warrior-aristocrats. With the daimyo gone, they also lost their source of income; their pensions, unlike those of the daimyo, were scarcely more than token sums. A small portion of them took up other livelihoods. Some became army officers or joined the police force. Many made good marriages into prosperous merchant families or took up a craft. A few secured positions of importance in government. But most disdained such lives and, as a result, were incapable of readjusting; they remained a disorgan-

ized threat to national stability.

When the government prohibited ex-samurai from wearing the traditional two swords by which their class had always been known, they rallied behind a leader by the name of Saigō Takamori. In 1877, he raised a rebellion in Satsuma and sent 150,000 ex-samurai against the new conscript army. He was killed in battle and his followers proved a poor match for the emperor's modernized citizen army. The uprising was the dying gasp of feudal Japan.

In other spheres, modernization was coming on with prodigious speed. Within the first decade of Meiji rule, Tokyo University was founded and a national education system set in motion. The first national bank was established and the first railway service between Tokyo and Yokohama was begun. A navy, a legal code, a telegraph network, and a West-

Nineteenth-century Japan remained largely a country of ancient beliefs and heroes. This print (above left) by Utagawa Kuniyoshi celebrates Nichiren, the militant priest who could not be threatened into submission. Above, Japanese diplomats embark on an unsuccessful mission to secure revisions of unequal treaties with the West.

ern-style calendar also were adopted. Foreign technicians were invited to advise the Japanese on industrial mechanization, on agricultural productivity, and on stimulating trade. The foundations for some of the great modern fortunes were laid as *zaibatsu,* or family-owned industrial cartels, became major economic forces in Japan. Western-style clothing, music, and architecture were increasingly popular.

One of the long-range goals of the leaders of the Meiji restoration was securing revisions of the un-

equal treaties which their predecessors had originally been forced to sign. To gain such revisions, it was necessary first to obtain international respect. One step in this direction, they believed, was the creation of a constitution. After eight years of preparation, Japan's first constitution was promulgated in 1889. Under the constitution, the emperor was legalized as an absolute, sacred monarch, above and outside the government, with ultimate authority in all matters. The Japanese people were his subjects. Advising the emperor was a privy council, a prime minister and a cabinet, ministers of the army and navy, and an assortment of other bureaucratic agencies directly responsible to the throne. The only concession to representative government was the bicameral legislature, the so-called Imperial Diet, which consisted of a House of Peers drawn from the old aristocratic classes and a lower house or parliament. Members of the latter were elected by a select minority of the population—just over one percent—who were qualified to vote. What limited advisory influence this parliament had on state matters was generally overruled by the more conservative Peers.

Though the constitution was extremely conservative by contemporary European standards, it represented a dramatic step forward in the Japanese political process. The Imperial Diet's influence was almost negligible in the beginning, but it did provide an arena for political debate and the growth of political parties. In time the government was forced to make numerous concessions to party pressures and to put limits on the oligarchic rule of its own executive branch.

One area in which the new government was consistently criticized by opposition leaders was in its relations with other Asian nations. The Meiji government had generally cast its lot with the pacifists among its numbers in the first two decades of its existence. The leader of the Satsuma Rebellion had previously left

Japan's war with China over suzerainty in Korea gave the West its first clear look at Japan's formidable new military machine. Japanese troops (above left) march through the gates of Seoul, the Korean capital, in 1894, as the Japanese government prepares to install a puppet on the throne. Left, a Japanese infantry meets the Chinese at P'yŏngyang. Japan's warships levy heavy casualties on the enemy in the Battle of Yalu (above right). Right, a counsel of war is held aboard a Japanese warship.

his post as a government counselor over a heated dispute concerning the merits of invading Korea, which the majority of counselors opposed. For some time afterward, the feeling among the oligarchs was that Japan had more pressing concerns than overseas expansion. But by the 1890s the gunboat diplomacy that the Western nations had so freely employed proved irresistible. The Japanese, intensely proud of their late accomplishments, felt ready to join the great powers in their own game.

Once again Korea became the focus of debate. China claimed suzerainty over the Korean peninsula, though Japan had gradually gained numerous trade concessions with the Korean government and resented China's presence there. War had been narrowly averted in 1885, but when China was asked by the Korean king to help put down a civil war within Korea's borders, the Japanese saw their opportunity to settle the matter to their advantage. The Japanese army swept into Seoul, the Korean capital, seized palace and king, installed its own puppet government, and ordered it to declare Korea's independence from China.

Japan then set about to expel Chinese troops, opening offensives on both land and sea, and in a matter of months had humbled this once great adversary. By the Treaty of Shimonoseki, signed in April 1895, China recognized Korean independence and ceded the Liaotung Peninsula, Formosa, and the Pescadores to Japan. If not for the intercessions of the now-alarmed governments of Germany, Russia, and France, Japan would have been able to retain the strategically important Liaotung Peninsula. With Russian warships menacing, however, the Meiji government was forced to relinquish this newly won mainland foothold.

The reaction of the Japanese people was one of profound anger. When the same Western nations that had chastised Japan proceeded to take some of the same lands for themselves, the Japanese began to mobilize for a second war. Rivalry with Russia grew particularly acute after the latter won a lease for the use of Port Arthur on the Liaotung Peninsula and made signs of involving itself in Korea. In 1904 Japanese ships surprized the Russian fleet at Port Arthur and defeated the Russian forces in the Tsushima Strait. Japan, the underdog, won itself numerous admirers for this decisive victory. A treaty signed in Portsmouth, New Hampshire, in 1905, yielded Russia's acknowledgement of Japan's supremacy in Korea and on the southern half of the island of Sakhalin, as well as the rights Japan had won and then lost on the Liaotung Peninsula a decade earlier.

Japan was now a major world power. When the greatly respected, much loved emperor Meiji died in 1912, the Japanese could declare themselves, for the first time in their history, a nation unified, with a common cause and a common identity. The consequences of that deliverance only time could tell.

Photography Credits

Index